YOUTHWORK

40 MORE READY-TO-USE MEETING GUIDES

YOUTHWORK

40 MORE READY-TO-USE MEETING GUIDES

by John Allan, Jenny Baker, Wendy Beech,
Jon Bicknell, Paul Borthwick, Danny Brierley,
John Buckeridge & Chris Curtis

Series Editor: John Buckeridge

KINGSWAY PUBLICATIONS

EASTBOURNE

ISBN 0 85476 660 X
Photos: Luke Golobitsh, Jonathan Mark
Illustrations: Ian Long, Simon Smith
Page design & additional illustrations: Tim Mountford

Designed and produced by Bookprint Creative Services, PO Box 827, BN21 3YJ, England
for KINGSWAY PUBLICATIONS, Lottbridge Drove, Eastbourne, East Sussex BN23 6NT
Printed in Great Britain.

YOUTHWORK 40 MORE READY-TO-USE MEETING GUIDES

CONTENTS

How to Use this Book

This material has been designed to be used with 11 to 16-year-olds. That doesn't mean it can't work with older teenagers — you'll just have to adapt it a little more. But since no two groups of young people are the same, you'll have to adapt and tweak some of the content anyway.

The five main themed sections in this book can be used in a year-long series, but will work just as well as individual units. You may find that some of the meeting outlines cover too much for just one week. The key thing is to adapt and personalise the material to take into account your own gifting, available resources and the needs of your young people.

Most of the units include icebreaker games, discussion starters and other interactive elements. It is important to avoid too much 'chalk and talk' style teaching. Young people learn best through a mix of learning elements.

You are free to photocopy the reproducible sheets for local church use. This does not apply to large-scale events where over 100 people are expected.

Please do prepare well. Although this book is designed to take some of the hard work and hassle out of preparation, you will still need to read through the meeting plan at least a couple of days beforehand. This will give you time to collect props, do background reading, and make copies of the repro-sheet.

My thanks go to my co-authors on this project — John Allan, Jenny Baker, Wendy Beech, Jon Bicknell, Paul Borthwick, Danny Brierley and Chris Curtis — for all their help and input.

Some of these meeting plans first appeared in YOUTHWORK magazine; however, they have been adapted and appear in this book for the first time with photocopiable worksheets. If you find this book helpful you're sure to be interested in YOUTHWORK magazine which publishes meeting plans, discussion starters and other meeting resources in every monthly issue.

If you haven't seen a copy of YOUTHWORK magazine, write to me for a sample copy. It is available from all good Christian bookshops, or if you would like to subscribe, turn to the advertisement on page 96 for more details.

John Buckeridge
Series Editor

YOUTHWORK, CCP, PO Box 17911,
London SW1E 5ZR
E-mail: bucks@globalnet.co.uk

SECTION 1
RELATIONSHIPS

Relationships are a subject any youth worker worth his or her salt will choose to regularly cover in your programming. As young people enter into the teenage years they live in a peculiar limbo world where they are neither fully children or fully adults. Often they will expect to be treated as adults and yet still enjoy children's activities and play. Physically their bodies are changing fast as hormones surge through their veins and as they mature sexually. This process can be alarming and stressful for both sexes. Often masturbation begins with accompanying guilt and confusion.

Some begin to date and experiment sexually. Read the agony columns of any teenage magazine and you will discover the issues they wrestle with at an increasingly younger age.

If your group is mixed I recommend that you split them into single sex groups for some parts of these meetings - particularly when you want them to honestly and candidly talk about relationship matters.

Finally, please don't imagine that if you use this series of meeting plans on relationships, that is 'it'. This is a theme you will need to revisit frequently over the next couple of years if you are to help young people to understand what the Bible teaches and if they are to be able to express their concerns, questions and opinions.

NEIGHBOURS

MEETING AIM: To help young people think about what makes a community a good place to live in and to help them see their role in the neighbourhood and what they can offer to make it a better place. Also to begin to explore their need for companionship with other people and God.

SPOT THE SOAP (15 mins)

Introduce the meeting by playing the theme tune (on a video or audio cassette) from *Neighbours*, the Aussie soap shown five days a week on BBC1. Encourage everyone to singalong with the tune. Say: 'This week the meeting is all about neighbours – not just those people who live next door, but the community we live in'.

Show the group some short videoed clips from these TV soaps (select two): *EastEnders*, *Neighbours*, *Coronation Street*, *Brookside*. Select sections which show the characters interacting in their community, eg at the market, café or Queen Vic pub in *EastEnders*.

Ask the group to choose a soap character they can identify with, either because they like them or think they have a similar attitude or personality. In turn ask each group member to share their choice and the reason behind it. Alternatively, do a 'Twenty Questions Quiz' to discover what soap character each person has chosen. Anyone can ask a question with a 'Yes' or 'No' answer, eg: 'Is your character from *Coronation Street*?' Up to twenty questions are allowed before the group has to guess their soap identity. The winner is the person(s) who remains undiscovered after twenty questions, or who took the most number of questions (up to twenty) before being successfully discovered.

As well as being fun, this exercise may reveal a few surprises about people's choices.

COMMUNITY DEFINED (3 mins)

Ask the group to suggest words or phrases that sum up the word 'community', also words that are often connected to community (eg, community centre). Write on an OHP or whiteboard some of the words or phrases suggested. After two minutes summarise the suggestions and then read out the following dictionary definition: 'Body of people living in the same locality; having things in common; a group unified by common interests.'

SIMTOWN (30 mins)

Hand out A2-size sheets of blank paper and pens/pencils, plus a photocopy of the page opposite and ask the group to work in small teams of twos or threes. Read out the task at the top of the Simtown sheet and explain that they have 15–20 minutes to design a town which would encourage a sense of community

among its inhabitants and be a place that they would like to live in.

After 15–20 minutes get the groups to display their Simtown maps and briefly explain them. Encourage questions and debate on the mix of housing,.

Q & A (15 mins)

Ask some or all of the following questions and get the young people in small groups or all together to discuss and study the Bible. The verses suggested are starting points and some groups may be able to find other verses or Scripture passages to bring more light to the question raised.

1) What is the solution to loneliness? Is it being with a large number of people or is it getting a few really close friends? Discuss, then check out Proverbs 18:24.

2) God made people and wants a relationship with us, but we are afraid of that – why? Discuss, then check out Genesis 3:8.

3) How is a relationship with God and eternal life made possible? Discuss, then check out John 3:16; Romans 6:5f.

4) Will being a Christian mean you never lack human friendship? Discuss, then check out Matthew 10:32–39.

5) Why is it important for Christians to meet together? Discuss, then check out Hebrews 10:25; 1 John 1:3–4.

6) Does God want us to befriend/help the lonely, poor, rejected, unloved and weaker members of society? Why? Discuss, then check out Matthew 25:31–46; Acts 20:35; 1 Thessalonians 5:14; Luke 10:25–37.

HOME ALONE (5–15 mins)

Say: 'In the film *Home Alone* Macaulay Culkin plays Kevin, the youngest son of a largish family who accidentally leave him behind when they leave home for a Christmas vacation. In the film Kevin copes with being alone really well, and even protects the home from burglars. However, if Kevin had been alone with little contact with other people for weeks on end, loneliness would have gripped him.

Lots of people feel alone, with no meaningful contact with other people. Spend a few minutes and make a list of the sorts of people (not individual names) who could be lonely. Remember they do not necessarily need to be living on their own to feel lonely.'

Give people a few moments to think and then ask them to call out their ideas (old people living on their own, single mums living in high-rise flats, refugees from abroad who have come to Britain to escape persecution, teenagers who don't belong to the 'in crowd' or who find it hard to make friends, etc). Compile a list on a whiteboard or OHP. When

you have a long list, go back through the list and ask for ideas to overcome the isolation or loneliness of these people groups.

For each listing, try to identify at least three solutions: one which could be as a result of the actions of the local or central government, one solution provided by the individuals themselves, and one resourced by individuals or groups with the church, youth group, or wider community. In particular get the group to brainstorm ways the youth group and/or church could get involved and make a positive difference in the community.

Having completed this exercise you may find a couple of ideas that the young people themselves thought of which they could actually do to make a difference to lonely or isolated people in your community. Spend some time talking this challenge through with them.

This exercise needs to be handled with tact and care – you do not want individuals in the youth group who are lonely or considered by others to be a 'misfit' to feel uncomfortable. You may find some of them contribute powerfully by sharing about their own feelings, but be careful – you do not want them to isolate themselves yet further by being embarrassed.

In addition you could contact the Social Services department of your local Council. Speak on the phone or arrange an appointment to meet with a member of staff there. Tell them about your youth group and ask for ideas on ways your young people can get involved in the local community.

One possible area of help and service is 'Adopt A Gran', linking two or three members of your youth group with an individual elderly person who may have no grandchildren living nearby. By regularly visiting the elderly person in their home or day centre to chat, play a game of cards, wash up, etc, young and old can benefit.

THE SAME BUT DIFFERENT

Read Exodus 23:23–24. Say: 'God warned the Israelites that if they lived in a place surrounded by people who worshipped other gods and followed different customs, they could easily adopt some of these practices and no longer be faithful to the God who led them into the land. It's the same for Christians living in a secular culture – we are surrounded by people who have different beliefs and values. God calls us to live a different way and to maintain a lifestyle that shows we are Christians.

'Part of that different lifestyle should be a caring attitude towards those members of our society who many others ignore, despise or treat unjustly.'

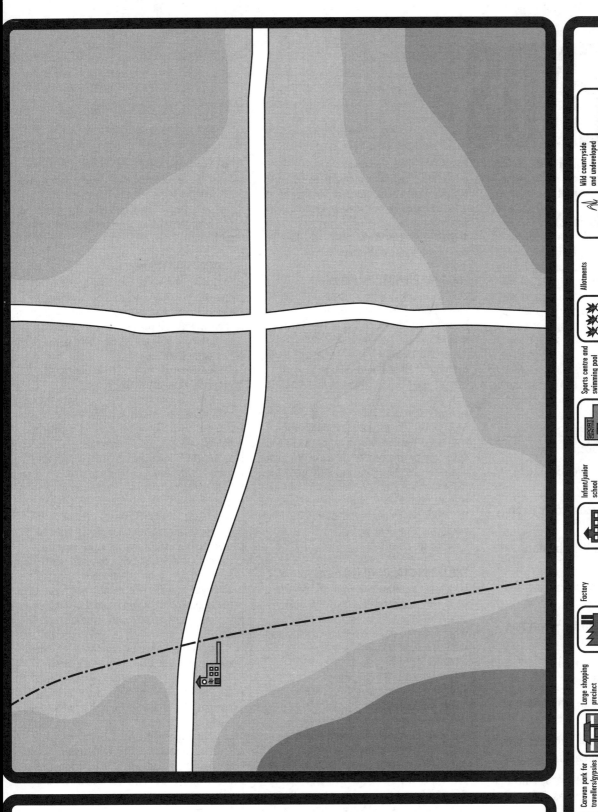

Sim Town

Design a simulated community which you would like to live in. Draw a map to illustrate your ideal town using the key symbols supplied. In particular you need to think about what sort or combination of housing there should be, low-price two-bedroom starter homes, mid-size council-owned housing, housing association flats, sheltered accommodation, large detached houses, etc. Also what parks, shopping developments, hotels, hospitals, factories, offices, etc (don't forget — no factories/offices means little employment for the population). Some facilities like a sewage farm or a prison may seem undesirable, but can your town do without them? Design too many leisure facilities and too few houses, and your sports hall or cinema will go out of business as there aren't enough people to use them to make them profitable! A railway line and some main roads are already included, but you'll need to decide where side roads go, or in fact if you want to restrict the amount of traffic by designing car parks at the end of each street to reduce residential traffic.

As well as being a nice place to live you need to be able to argue that your Simtown is practical and workable. If there is a facility/building that you want to include that isn't on the key, just design a symbol to represent it (you are allowed to add up to six additional symbols), add it to the key and then draw it on your map. You do not need to include every symbol from the key. If you don't want any schools in your town that's up to you, but you will need to defend your decision to the rest of the group as your task is not only to make this a town you want to live in, — but one for other people also.

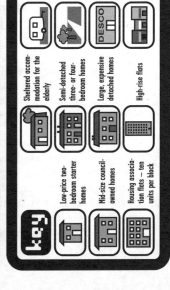

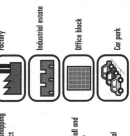

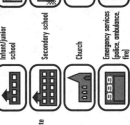

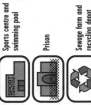

FRIENDS

MEETING AIM: To explore the meaning of friendship, apply biblical principles to it, and encourage the group to befriend people who need their friendship.

THAT'S YOU, THAT IS (10 mins)
Give everyone a photocopy of the diagram (right). This is a picture of their social lives – they have to fill names in the spaces. (Really close friends may like to work together on this; that's fine.) After completing it, they need not show the results, but get them to keep it safely, they'll need this sheet again before the meeting ends.

FIND YOUR SOULMATE (10 mins)
Why do people make friends with one another? Give each of the group a name label to wear, saying things like:

Jamie, 15, who lives in Little Muttering (pop. 350).

Richard, 15, who lives in Little Muttering (pop. 350).

Alison, 13, who is extremely keen on tennis.

Fiona, 13, who is a Wimbledon regular.

Kevin, 16, who thinks Andrew is wonderful.

Andrew, 17, who thinks Kevin has very good taste.

Rachel, 15, who is outgoing, attractive and confident.

Anne, 15, who is pale, shy and a little overweight.

Alan, 16, from Bristol, who went to a boys' camp in Lancashire last year.

Donald, 16, from Inverness, who went to the same camp as Alan.

Eric, 17, who has memorised the Inter City timetable and has a favourite blue anorak.

Ask them to circulate and find the person with whom they would be most likely to form a friendship. Warn them that they may not find anyone! After they have paired up, investigate the results.

Ask: Why this person? What reason would there be for bonding in this case? Does it always work this way? (eg, two boys living in a small rural village could be deadly enemies.) Did anyone not find a friend, and if so why? Are some people less likely to form friendships than others, and if so, whose fault is it?

Points that should emerge:
● We make friendships for various reasons.
● Sometimes shared interests or experiences draw us together, but sometimes, too, 'opposite poles attract'.
● Making friends is a skill; it's possible to repel people unconsciously.

WHAT IS FRIENDSHIP? (10 mins)
Look at one of these case studies (or all, by dividing into small sub-groups):
● David and Jonathan (1 Sam 18:1–4; 19:1–7)
● Barnabas and Paul (Acts 9:26–28; 11:19–26; 15:36–40)
● Ruth and Naomi (Ruth 1:3–5; 11–18)

ASK:
● What happens in this story that shows true friendship? How do the same things happen nowadays? Have they ever happened to you?
● Did the people concerned make any mistakes – or did they do things differently from the way you would have behaved?
● If you had to write one sentence based on this story, which began 'Friendship is…', how would you complete it?

Compare results…

THE JESUS STANDARD (10 mins)
Look at 1 Corinthians 13:4–7 and say : 'If we're Christians, this is how we should behave to others – including our friends. What does this passage tell us we should and shouldn't do to them?'

You could make this more specific:
● How would this passage apply if your friend had found a new boyfriend and just wasn't seeing you any more?
● If you found a new boyfriend?
● If your friend told somebody else a secret you'd confided in him?
● If your friend owed you money and didn't pay you back?
● If your friend accused you of something, then wouldn't speak to you again?
● If you knew your friend had done something illegal?
● If your friend was taking drugs?'

YOU'VE GOT A FRIEND (10 mins)
How do people make friendships? In small groups, list ten ways not to do it, ie behaviour that will put other people off. (Get them to think of people at school who haven't got many friends. What are they doing wrong?)

Ask them to choose one item from their list and role-play it to the other groups.

After you've watched the role plays, discuss:
● If these are ways not to do it, do they give us any clues about techniques which can be effective?

● How would Jesus have reacted if he had been on the receiving end of these approaches?

How did Jesus react to friendless and unlovely people (eg, Zacchaeus, the woman at the well, the woman who anointed his feet with ointment etc)?

CONCLUSION (10 mins)
In this session we've explored a little of how and why we make friends. For most people this is an unconscious process, based solely on their whims and prejudices. For Christians, with the life of Jesus inside, there needs to be two extra elements:

1) A determination to treat our friends properly, with Jesus' love.

2) An outgoing willingness to make friends with those who others just don't want to know. It isn't cool and it wins no popularity points, but it's what Jesus wants.

Ask them to go back to the diagram they drew at the beginning. Get them to look carefully at the names in the two outer circles: 'People who aren't my friends' and 'People who aren't anybody's friends'. Either on their own or together with their closest friends, get them to discuss for five minutes what they could do that would begin to reach out to some of those people with whom they just don't get on well. Which ones most need their friendship? What action could they take? You may need to be ready with some suggestions here.

Stress that only they can decide whether to apply any of the ideas they have generated. But if they truly want other people to discover the love of Christ, perhaps they could take just one idea and work on it that week, then report back to the group the following week on what happened.

Close in prayer, asking God to make us sensitive to the friends we have, and courageous in reaching out to others we aren't friends with yet.

ALL CHANGE!

MEETING AIM: To help young people to understand what is happening to their bodies during puberty and to appreciate the opposite sex and the changes occurring to them a little better as well.

PICTURE PEOPLE (5 mins)

Put the group into pairs and hand out paper, pencils and felt-tipped pens. Tell the pairs to sit opposite each other and to draw their partner's face. Tell them they have five minutes to create an accurate representation of their partner.

However, after just one or two minutes call a halt to their drawings. The idea is to ensure that most of them have not completed their drawing.

Compare drawings, allowing some laughter and indignation, then settle the group down and make the following points:

● Not every drawing is complete because not enough time was given for them to be finished.

● Those few drawings that were finished are not necessarily the best drawings – as some of the incomplete ones are likely to be more admired once they are complete.

● In the same way that the drawings are incomplete, so young people who are going through puberty are not the finished article. Just as the drawings were at different stages of completion, so the members of this group are developing at different rates and are at different stages.

SHOE PEOPLE (5 mins)

Ask everyone to take off their shoes and throw them into a pile in the middle of the room. Explain that when you say 'go' they need to grab a pair of shoes that are not their own and put them on. The pairs don't even need to be matching. Play this game a couple of times.

Say: 'Putting on someone else's shoes can be painful if they're too small, and uncomfortable if they're smelly or sweaty. This awkward feeling is a little bit like the feelings most people experience as they approach, enter and go through puberty. Some people say they feel like they're not really in their own body any more – it's changed and it feels rather strange and awkward. For others the feelings of embarrassment at puberty are because they're one of the last people in their class at school or youth group at church who haven't yet grown breasts or started to grow facial hair.'

HELP OR HURT? (10 mins)

Hand out paper and pens and then in groups of two or threes ask the young people to make a list under two headings 'help' and 'hurt'. Underneath each heading ask the groups to list words and deeds that either 'help' other people who are going through puberty or 'hurt' them. Give them an example or two to get them going, eg calling someone 'crater face' if they are spotty could be put under 'hurt'…

Feed back the lists and encourage discussion on 'helping' each other in the group, or younger brothers/sisters entering puberty, by being sensitive to them.

CHANGEATHON (10 mins)

Split the sexes and get the lads and girls to form groups of two or three. Hand each small group a pen and a A5 piece of paper. Then ask them to list the physical and emotional changes that affect members of the opposite sex as they pass through puberty.

Expect a bit of giggling and embarrassment at first, but encourage them to complete this task. Then collect in the papers and read out what the lads identified happens to girls and vice versa. List these on a whiteboard or OHP and use the list below to correct or add to their information.

Get the groups to discuss and feed back on the following questions:

● Which comments that the opposite sex listed did they get right/wrong and which surprised you?

● Which changes/feelings do both sexes have in common?

● Give examples of the ways girls and boys differ as they go through puberty and into teenage years.

● In what areas do you wish the opposite sex would be more sensitive about the way your sex is and feels? (This last question could lead into an extension of the earlier discussion on sensitivity and understanding of the opposite sex. Be prepared to give this extra time and then discuss plenty.)

CHANGEATHON

Male	Female
● Body grows to full height	● Body grows to full height
● Penis grows	● Breasts grow
● Voice gets deeper	● Periods begin
● Body hair grows	● Body hair grows
● Skin gets oilier	● Skin gets oilier
● Sudden mood/ emotion swings	● Sudden mood/ emotion swings
● Increasing sexual desires	● Increasing sexual desires
● Facial hair grows	● Hips become wider
● Increased self-consciousness	● Increased self-consciousness

AGONY AUNT/UNCLE (15–20 mins)

Get your youngsters into single sex groups of two or three and give each group a photocopy of the appropriate half of the page opposite (agony aunt letter for girls, agony uncle letter for lads).

Each group should compose a letter with three pieces of advice which could include a biblical perspective.

Allow up to ten minutes for work in the groups and then ask for feedback.

During the feedback ask the opinions of each sex of the others' problem and how they dealt with it.

N.B. The quality of this activity will partly depend on how well you have prepared.

Make sure you have a female helper available to assist the girls' groups and a male helper for the lads' groups. They need to think through both agony letters beforehand, having considered the various ideas, arguments and advice that the groups may come up with.

Also think through the likely questions they may have and have a number of Bible references to give to the groups for feedback discussion if needed (eg, Jeremiah 9:23–24 – a perspective on our basis for self-respect; Proverbs 11:25 – the value of a kind word; 1 Samuel 16:7 – people look on the outward appearance but God looks at the heart).

GUIDED MEDITATION (5 mins)

Play some 'mood' music, eg a track from *The Celts* album by Enya, some Taizé-style worship or some ambient music.

Encourage everyone to close their eyes and relax. Then while the music continues, slowly read aloud Psalm 139:13–16. Leave frequent pauses during the reading.

Conclude the meeting by praying a prayer of thanks to God for making each of us, knowing all about us and loving us. Pray that as a result of this week's meeting we will all be more sensitive and caring about the way others feel about their appearance.

Dear Agony Aunt

I'm 14, but compared to all my mates who are 14 I look like an 11-year-old! I hate it at break and lunch times at school because some of the lads call me names and make fun of my flat chest. Most of the girls in my class are OK, although I know some of them snigger at me when we change for PE or swimming. I haven't started having periods yet, but when I try to explain how I feel to my mum she just tells me I'm a late developer, to be glad that I haven't got the hassle of periods, and not to worry. But I do worry and I hate the way I look.

The other day a new teacher called me over and asked why I wasn't in the hall for assembly with the rest of Year 7. What made it worse was that the class joker, Sammy Jones, heard it and told everyone.

My older sister has just started at university, so I can't even tell her.

From Siobhan

Dear Agony Uncle

I'm 14 and I hate my body. I'm tall but I'm really thin. My real name is Neil, but my nickname at school is 'Matchstick' or 'Stick Insect' which I hate, but I pretend it doesn't bother me. My older brother Shaun is 18 and he's good looking and has a really muscly body. He has a gorgeous girlfriend. Shaun goes to the local gym for bodybuilding four nights a week with his mate Dave. I told them I'd like to go too but Shaun laughed his head off and told me they don't allow people from concentration camps to attend because it would be bad for their image. A week later Dave told me he could get me some steroid tablets which build up muscle bulk with hardly any work. He reckons they only cost £15 for a bottle of 24 tablets and that loads of people take them – including Shaun!

What do you reckon?

From Neil

Dear Siobhan…

_____
_____
_____
_____
_____
_____
_____
_____
_____
_____
_____
_____
_____
_____
_____
_____
_____
_____
_____

Dear Neil…

_____
_____
_____
_____
_____
_____
_____
_____
_____
_____
_____
_____
_____
_____
_____

JUST GOOD FRIENDS

MEETING AIM: To take a biblical look at the expectations we have of courtship rituals – dating, breaking up, getting serious – and work out how Christian convictions should affect our behaviour.

FATAL ATTRACTION (15 mins)

Begin by showing a short clip from a film such as *Clueless*, where a hapless girl is being pushed into going out with someone who is completely wrong for her. (Failing this, look for a short clip from *Neighbours*, *Home and Away* or *Brookside* which deals with dating agonies – there's at least one every episode!) Use this to launch the question: how do we know who we should go out with? More teenage agony and energy is expended on this than almost any other subject. Songs, films and magazines are almost entirely devoted to it. (You could bring along a teenage girls' magazine to make your point...)

Gone are the days when your first romantic encounter would probably be your only one. Most people in today's society have a variety of liaisons before they find the right person for them. So how do we find that person? And how do we behave while we're finding them?

Divide the group into a number of 'dating agencies'. Let them choose a suitably cheesy name for their company, if they wish. Then give each agency a photocopy of the sheet opposite, which contains five application forms. Ask each group to write a description of the perfect partner for each of these people. After five minutes, compare results, and use the results to answer the questions below:

● How did you decide what the partner should be like? What makes one person attracted to another?
● Was there anyone for whom you really couldn't imagine finding a partner? Why?
● Did you have enough information to be able to make good suggestions? What else would it be important to know about your clients?

FAST LOVE? (10 mins)

Now get the group to vote on whether they agree or disagree with these statements.

'There is no such thing as love at first sight.'

'There is one perfect person for you, and if you miss this person, your life will never be complete.'

'The person you love is the one you feel the strongest emotions for.'

'You should never go out with someone unless you are absolutely sure you care for them deeply.'

'The Bible says you should never kiss on the first date.'

You will probably have quite a variety of opinions expressed! Sum up by pointing out:

1) It's possible to feel really strongly for someone at first encounter, and this may eventually turn into love, but real love means knowing a person intimately – bad bits as well as good – and still caring.

2) If there is just one pre-ordained partner for you (and the Bible never says so), God will make sure you will find this person and will have no doubts about it, so relax!

3) Love may involve strong emotions, but there's more to love than that – emotions can be extremely deceptive.

4) It's possible for two people to go out together for all sorts of reasons, not just romantic involvement.

5) The Bible says nothing about dating, because marriage arrangements then were very different from those of our Western society.

GOD ON DATING (10 mins)

So if the situation was so different, can the Bible really help? Yes, because it gives us principles we can apply. Do a little Bible study. Write up on an OHP acetate or flipchart:

PRINCIPLES FOR DATING
● *The kind of people we should be*
● *The way we should treat one another*
● *The way people who are dating should treat other friends*
● *Why boys and girls go out together anyway*
● *The meaning of real love*

Give each 'dating agency' paper and a pen, and a list of verses: James 3:17; 1 Corinthians 6:18–20; Philippians 2:3–4; 2 Timothy 2:22; Philippians 3:14; 1 John 3:18; Hebrews 13:4; James 1:19; 1 Corinthians 13:4-5; Matt 19:4–6.

Say that each verse gives some information about one of these topics. Ask them to find out what it is, and where it fits.

RULES FOR ROMANCE (10 mins)

Review your results. If these are some of the principles, how do they work in practice? Look together at some case studies, and decide what would be the biblical thing to do in each case...

● Susie is driving the boys mad. She is very attractive and extremely popular, but she never seems to go out with anybody more than a couple of times. She has been out with half of the group now, and each time it looks promising, but then suddenly she drops the boy and goes off with someone else. She says she just doesn't want to get too friendly with anyone, and she can't understand why they get so hurt.

● Ben and Will aren't speaking. At a party last month, Ben had a blazing row with his long-term girlfriend, Claire, and stomped off home. After cooling down, he came back, only to find his best friend Will had taken advantage of the situation and had already monopolised Claire for himself. Now Will and Claire are going out, and although Ben knows that she's just doing it to get back at him, he feels like murdering both of them.

● Julie has broken up with Sam. She says that if he's supposed to be a Christian, how come he can't keep his hands off her? Sam feels hurt, because she seemed to be enjoying their passionate moments as much as he was, and he thinks it's just an excuse. He is also not pleased that she has told all the details of their relationship to her friends. Should he have it out with her, or plead with her to have him back?

● Anna's friends are very worried about her. She is going out with a boy who is really attractive, but he is not a Christian and is well known as a casual supplier of soft drugs. Anna insists that she knows exactly what she's doing, and that she won't compromise her principles for anyone, but she hasn't been to the youth group once in the last three weeks, and she does seem to have been to a lot of dodgy parties. What should they do?

BREAKING UP GRACEFULLY (15 mins)

Finally, if we decide it's time to call it a day, how should we end a relationship? Ask each group to think of three terrible ways of doing it badly, and then to role-play them in front of the others. Watch the results, and sum up.

Breaking up needs to be done gently, with real concern for the other person. It needs to be honest, with an open statement of the real reasons involved. It should be face to face – (the England cricketer who sent his wife a fax to terminate their marriage was not a Christian!) It must be firm, not allowing the other person to think there's still hope where there is none. It must be non-confrontational – it's easy to mask your embarrassment by picking a quarrel with the person you're about to dump, but that isn't fair. And it must be done with a concern to save the relationship – after the hurt is over, you should still be able to respect one another and even be friends.

If there's time, get the group to think about the other side: what principles should you observe if you're the one who's been dumped (eg, not reacting with hatred; not becoming a nuisance, and refusing to take 'no' for an answer; not spreading stories about your former partner; not going immediately into a 'rebound' relationship, just to retaliate)?

Finally sum up with: dating is a tricky area, and the way human emotions work is extremely complex (Proverbs 30:18-19). But God has given us some clues about how we can make our way through the minefield without hurting others or ourselves. We need to keep them in view!

the dating agency

CHOOSE A SUITABLY CHEESY NAME FOR YOUR DATING AGENCY. YOUR TASK IS TO WRITE A DESCRIPTION OF THE PERFECT PARTNER FOR EACH OF THESE FIVE PEOPLE WHO HAVE APPLIED TO YOUR AGENCY. YOU HAVE FIVE MINUTES TO COMPLETE THIS EXERCISE.

ALEX, 17, IS INTERESTED IN TRAINSPOTTING AND COLLECTING MARMALADE LABELS. HE HAS TWO GCSES AND IS A SHELF-STACKER IN TESCO'S. ALEX IS NOT GOOD AT MAKING FRIENDS.

ALEX'S IDEAL PARTNER IS . . . .

. . . .

. . . .

DEBBIE, 16, IS INTERESTED IN CLUBBING AND COSMETICS. SHE HAS SEVEN GCSES AND IS A TRAINEE HAIRDRESSER ON DAY RELEASE AT SIXTH FORM COLLEGE. DEBBIE IS EASILY BORED.

DEBBIE'S IDEAL PARTNER IS . . . .

. . . .

. . . .

ROWENA, 20, IS INTERESTED IN SNOWBOARDING AND RALLY DRIVING. SHE HAS SEVEN GCSES AND TWO A-LEVELS TO SHOW FROM HER EDUCATION AT AN EXCLUSIVE GIRLS' BOARDING SCHOOL. SHE IS NOW A GIRL FRIDAY FOR A RECORD PRODUCER.

ROWENA'S IDEAL PARTNER IS . . . .

. . . .

. . . .

GARETH, 16, IS A KEEN FOOTBALLER AND KEEP-FIT FANATIC. WHEN HE ISN'T PLAYING FOOTBALL HE IS WATCHING SPORTS ON SATELLITE TV OR WORKING OUT AT THE GYM. HE HAS FIVE GCSES AND IS ABOUT TO TAKE HIS A-LEVELS. HE HOPES TO GO ON TO UNIVERSITY TO TRAIN AS A P.E. TEACHER.

GARETH'S IDEAL PARTNER IS . . . .

KIM, 18, IS INTERESTED IN COOKERY AND READING ROMANTIC OR HISTORICAL NOVELS. SHE HAS EIGHT GCSES AND TWO A-LEVELS AND IS TRAINING TO BECOME AN ACCOUNTANT. SHE IS SHY AND FINDS IT HARD TO SOCIALISE.

KIM'S IDEAL PARTNER IS . . . .

. . . .

. . . .

LET'S TALK ABOUT SEX

MEETING AIM: To get young people talking about sex. To teach that sex is a gift which was created by God – not Haagen Dazs ice cream! To illustrate how sex is portrayed in adverts, popular music, teen magazines etc, and how that image and underlying philosophy are very different from the way God intended for us to understand and enjoy sex.

PREPARATION

Beforehand you will need to buy a selection of teenage magazines and collect a range of other glossy magazines. You also need to tape record ten current chart songs about love/sex and record onto video a collection of TV adverts which use sexy images to help sell a product. Other materials/resources required are: TV and video, cassette player, large sheets of cardboard, glue, scissors, blank paper, pens, Bibles and photocopies of the worksheet opposite.

NAME THAT SONG (10 mins)

Record short clips from ten current chart songs which include lyrics about love and/or sex. Hand out paper and pens and play the clips one at a time, allowing a few seconds' thinking time for them to identify the band and song before playing the next clip. Once all ten have been played, rewind the tape and play them through again, identifying the band and song. Give a suitable prize to the winning individuals or groups.

Say: 'The subject of love and sex is a recurring theme in popular music. The lyrics often focus on desire, wanting, asking for forgiveness, requests to stay the night, love me more, etc. This week we'll be looking at how love, and sex in particular, is portrayed in popular culture and the media.'

FRONT COVERS (5 mins)

Put them into small groups of three or four and hand each group a copy of the current issue of a teenage girls' magazine, a different magazine for each group (eg, *Bliss, Sugar, J17, More!, Minx*). Ask the group to read just the front cover of the magazine and discuss the images and words used.

Get each group to feed back their reaction to the cover and the reasons why they think each magazine editor has chosen the images and words.

In 1996 Marketing Week magazine commented on the circulation war between teenage girls' magazines, highlighting that editors are using more editorial about sex as one of the main strategies to try and win more readers. 'Sex sells' seems to be the strategy. Ask the groups to look again at their magazine and circle with a pen any words or images with a sexual link.

The chances are that many of the magazines will be liberally marked/circled. Hold each one up in turn and point out the way the magazine is using sex to sell their magazine.

MORE SEX TODAY? (15 mins)

Ask your group to answer these questions, then discuss the opinions raised. You may need to be prepared to throw in some opinions in order to spark debate.

● Is sex talked about more now than when your parents were teenagers? Is that a good or bad thing?
● Is sex education more available and informative now than when your parents were teenagers? Is that a good or a bad thing?
● Is sex portrayed in films, magazines adverts, etc in a more explicit way now than when your parents were teenagers?
● Where should young people get most of their information about sex from?
● Where do young people get most of their information about sex from? Discuss.
● Adverts, films, etc often use very explicit sexual images. How do you think this affects children, teenagers, adults? Do they affect men in different ways to women? Discuss.

SEX AND ADVERTISING (20 mins)

Hand out a pile of magazines which should include teenage magazines (eg, *J17*), women's magazines (eg, *Cosmopolitan*), men's magazines (eg, *GQ*), style magazines (eg, *The Face*). Ask your young people to rip out ads which use sex or sexy images to help sell a product. Stick these onto several large pieces of card until you have quite a collection. Then get the young people to call out the products which the sexy images are being used to advertise. Write a list of the products onto an OHP or whiteboard.

Encourage discussion on the different ways that sexual images were used in ads (shock factor, turn-on factor, trying to give a boring product more appeal, etc).

'Sex is a powerful driving force in us all. Companies recognise this and use distorted sexual images for their own commercial gain. In the process they cheapen sex and women in particular.'

Discuss the statement above. Is it right, overstated and oversimplified, or wrong?

In small groups ask the young people to think of alternative strategies to sex to help promote ice cream, cars or deodorant (eg, humour, factual).

Then show a selection of TV ads which you have pre-videoed, and get the group to vote on their favourite and to discuss why they thought the ad was a good one, what selling tactics were used and why.

LET'S TALK… (10+ mins)

The worksheet opposite is an optional section of this week's programme. This discussion-provoking visual with questions will prompt lots of discussion in some groups and embarrassed silence in others – it depends on the chemistry of the group. With more mature and vocal young people these statements and questions will provide enough discussion and debate for a whole session. You may like to ask some young people or adults beforehand specifically to address one of the questions/issues raised on the sheet.

GOD AND SEX (20 mins)

Write the list of words and Bible references below onto a whiteboard or OHP:
● power ● pleasure ● gentle ● disappointment ● fondness ● exploitation ● cheap thrills ● tender ● selfish pleasure ● tasteful ● soft porn ● love ● lust ● affection ● cheap ● beautiful ● tacky ● soft ● passion ● devotion ● loyalty ● hunger ● temporary ● guilt ● care ● lasting ● faithful ● casual ● Proverbs 5:18–20 ● Proverbs 5:23–29 ● 1 Thessalonians 4:3–8 ● Song of Songs 2:1; 4:1–7 ● Mark 10:9 ● 1 Corinthians 6:18 ● Exodus 20:14

Get the group into twos or threes then hand out a pen, paper and Bible. Ask each small group to take another look at the magazine adverts you collected and pasted onto card earlier. Each of these ads used sex to help sell their product. From the list of words on the OHP, discuss and then list those words which the group consider apply to the way that sex is portrayed in these ads.

Allow a couple of minutes for this and then ask the groups to look up the Bible references and write a mini-summary of each passage. Then ask them to compare the words listed with the Bible summaries. What conclusions can you draw from this?

Help them to see the significance of the vastly different attitudes towards sex portrayed in ads and what Scripture says is God's ideal.

Conclude by highlighting that:
● Sex is created by God (Genesis 1:27).
● Sex is a cause for joy and celebration (Song of Solomon 6:3). Make the point that the Bible contains a lengthy and sensuous love song (Song of Solomon) between a man and his wife. The song of the lovers contains exotic descriptions of their spontaneous feelings for each other and the pleasure and joy of their relationship. God is not anti-sex – he did create it after all!
● Sex is pure within a marriage (Hebrews 13:4).

PORNOGRAPHY

MEETING AIM: To get the group to reflect on why pornography affects us, and what God says we should do about it.

Be careful about displaying material, or even listening to group members' anecdotes – as you could be causing serious problems to somebody sitting quietly in the corner! And be ready to do some personal counselling as a result of the issues raised.

INTRODUCTION (10 mins)

Put up on the wall a 'picture gallery' of 15 numbered photographs cut from magazines. Give each person a piece of paper and a pencil, and ask them to browse in the gallery for five minutes, noting down the number of any pictures which really attract or excite them. The pictures should be a mixture of landscapes, flashy consumer items, eg, motorbikes, fashion accessories, or computer gear, but there must be at least one picture of an attractive boy and one of a beautiful girl.

Compare results afterwards. You will usually find that some are attracted by computers, bikes, sports pictures, etc, depending on their interests, but nearly everybody is attracted by the human being – if they're being honest, anyway!

Now ask them to turn the paper over and draw something they have seen many times before – a five pound note. They are not allowed to look at a real one. Promise a small box of chocolates as a prize for the best attempt.

When you have selected the best (usually the results are hilarious!), present the prize – a picture of a box of chocolates. After some protests, but before they lynch you, hand over the real thing.

Point out that this strange exercise has highlighted three simple points:

(a) All of us respond powerfully to pictures of people we're attracted to.

(b) There are some things we can see again and again without really noticing. There are other things which immediately jolt our attention into action.

(c) A picture sometimes is no substitute for the real thing.

WHAT ARE WE TALKING ABOUT? (10 mins)

Say that tonight we're talking about pornography – an industry which relies on using pictures, film and words to evoke a powerful response in us, and so shift millions of pounds every year. Sex grabs attention.

But where does pornography begin and end? Ask the group to vote on which of these are 'definitely porn', 'borderline' or 'definitely not porn':

(a) Page 3 of *The Sun*

(b) *Playboy* magazine

(c) The D.H. Lawrence novel *Lady Chatterley's Lover*

(d) The lyrics to a song by Prince (to use his former name)

(e) A Jackie Collins novel

(f) Mills and Boon's *Temptations* series

(g) The Sunday Sport

(h) Picasso's *Blue Nude*

(i) The video *Hot and Horny in Amsterdam*

You may (I hope!) have to explain a little about the contents of some of these, so if they're not familiar to you (I made (i) up!) you may wish to substitute other examples. To take along a copy of the Sun, a reproduction of the Picasso painting, and the Prince lyrics could be helpful.

Discuss your conclusions. There will probably be some agreement. One point should emerge: the borderlines are blurred. Some people claim to be unaffected by things which others find extremely hard to cope with. So the important question is not 'What is pornography?' in the abstract, but 'What is bad for me?' We have to be really honest about what is, and is not, harmful to us, and to avoid anything we're unsure about.

THE TROUBLE WITH PORN (10 mins)

Read the story below. It's about someone who is seriously weird, but if they substitute 'sex' for 'jelly babies' it may give them some ideas about why pornography is dangerous.

If you handle it properly, this might give rise to discussion about increasing obsession; waste of time and money; inadequate social skills, and inability to relate to other people; the hint of a link to violence; the devaluing of other people; the growing need for more; and so on.

Make it clear that not every porn user will end up like the jelly baby freak! But those are the trends which can set into someone's life when this kind of obsession takes hold.

WHAT THE BIBLE SAYS (15–20 mins)

Now divide into smaller groups, and give each group a photocopy of the worksheet opposite and a pen and Bible. Give them five to seven minutes to work through the list of questions and verses.

Then compare results. Don't just give the right answers; spend some time discussing what the verses really say. (A vital part of your preparation for this meeting may be some in-depth Bible study of these passages first.)

Close in prayer, asking God to help us discern honestly what is evil for us, and to keep our minds protected from harm.

'I really love jelly babies. When I can't afford to buy any, I cut the advertisements out of magazines and just look at them. I love to imagine what it would be like to gobble them all up. I've got some great Bassett's posters on the walls of my room – cost me a fortune, but then they bring me so much pleasure. In fact I don't go out much; I tend just to sit at home and look at my jelly baby posters. I do find it a bit difficult spending time with people anyway. It's hard to be interested in the kinds of things they're interested In. All I think about when I meet them is: what kind of jelly babies do they like best? I find myself thinking a lot about how they would eat them, and how often they have them.

'I wasn't always this interested in jelly babies. I suppose you could call it an interest which has grown. I can't concentrate on my job much; I find myself dreaming about jelly babies instead. I like to look on myself as a connoisseur of beautiful things. I just want to own them for myself; I can't bear the thought of jelly babies that don't belong to me. Some nights, when I can't afford any, I get so desperate I could go down to the local sweet shop and smash a window. I've often fantasised about doing it, but I don't suppose I ever will.'

Fill in the names of people who fit into these different categories

PEOPLE I KNOW
WHO AREN'T
ANYBODY'S FRIENDS

PEOPLE I KNOW WHO
AREN'T MY FRIENDS

OTHER
FRIENDS

MY CLOSE
FRIENDS

ME

PORN
What the Bible says...

Look up these Bible passages and then match up each question with the verse which helps to answer it. Draw a line between each matched verse and question.

1) Galatians 6:1

2) James 5:16

3) James 1:13–15

4) 1 Corinthians 10:13

5) Romans 12:2

a) How do I control the evil thoughts that pornography feeds on?

b) What can God do for me when I'm tempted?

c) Why does God tempt me anyway?

d) How can I get help to stand against temptation?

e) How do I help somebody else who has problems in this area?

HOMOSEXUALITY

MEETING AIM: This is a big and complex subject, partly because it's so intimate, and may well have a direct personal relevance to one or two of your group, and you too. This is such a 'hot potato' in the media today, so the aim of this outline is restricted to: (a) increasing the group's awareness of the issues that are being debated; (b) giving them a little more factual information on the subject; (c) helping them wrestle with what Scripture says on the issue; (d) developing sensitivity towards homosexual and lesbian people.

Watch your group's reactions to this session. You may want to have a further, personal chat with some of them if you suspect that they are troubled by their sexual orientation, or if you feel their attitudes are unbiblical and need a little more confrontation. You may well find that this session throws up so many issues that you need to run a further one.

HUMAN RESISTANCE FRONT (20–25 mins)

Divide the group into sub-groups of five. Ask them to pretend that the earth has been conquered by aliens from Alpha Centauri who have turned humans into slaves, killed millions and raped thousands of women. You are attending a meeting of a secret cell of the Human Resistance Front, where you are hammering out your plans to begin striking back. Each person will be given a card containing instructions for the part they have to play. They must show this card to no one else.

Then give each group an envelope containing five cards which are to be distributed to group members at random. The cards say:

1. You are a former professional soldier whose wife was raped by the Centaurans, then thrown out to die. You want to wage guerrilla warfare against them by any means possible. Anyone with a drop of Centauran blood must die. You are especially scornful of half-breeds, the product of shameful liaisons between Centaurans and human women. You think they are unnatural abominations and must be found and executed.

2. You are a former vicar who believes that Earth must fight back, but you're not sure how violent we have to be. You don't hate Centaurans, although you are shocked by their savagery.

3. You are a former National Front Leader to whom it's quite simple. Centaurans are another race. They've got to die. And any of their half-breeds must be killed off too – for the purity of the race.

4. You are a former school teacher with pacifist views. You want to resist the invaders, but without causing death and destruction. You believe that if the Front caused enough havoc and unrest by sabotaging Centauran homes and military outposts, they would go away.

5. You are a keen Earth patriot, but you have a secret which nobody knows. Your mother was a Centauran girl who fell in love with your human father. Both parents are now dead and everybody assumes you are fully human too. You want Earth to be free, but you don't want the Centaurans to be hurt in the process. You can admit your identity to the group if you think you can trust them, but it may be dangerous.

Let the groups hold their discussions for seven or eight minutes, then call them together. Ask the No. 5s to stand up and identify themselves. Read out what their card says. Then ask:

- How did it feel being a No. 5?
- How did the others react to them?
- Did anyone guess their secret?
- If so, what happened when they 'came out'?
- Did any of them lie about their real identity?
- How does the group feel about them now?

Explain that this is a kind of picture of the dilemma faced by young people who find that they are growing up different from others where their sexuality is concerned. It's easy to feel excluded or panicky – or even bitter, because you didn't ask to be this way. You end up constantly asking yourself, 'Who can I trust to talk to about it?' It's worse when you hear people making casual jokes about people like you, and talking quite ignorantly.

In 1948 Alfred Kinsey's report on male sexuality (now widely discredited) claimed that there were many more homosexually oriented people than anyone had dreamed. Homosexuals weren't just a tiny minority of perverts; they were a significant minority. Since then, as the laws controlling homosexual practice have gradually been relaxed, the homosexual community has gained the courage to come more and more into the spotlight, calling for centuries of oppression to come to an end. So today one of the most pressing problems the church must address is: What do we do about it? What is a biblical attitude to take?

GLAD TO BE GAY (5 mins)

Remind the group of just how prevalent 'gay' ideas and images are in society today, perhaps playing snatches of records by outspokenly homosexual or bisexual artistes (eg, Erasure, Boy George, Elton John, David Bowie, kd lang).

Show them some articles from recent newspapers, or run video clips from films in which gay characters appear prominently. Get the group to list as many prominent people as they can who are openly homosexual.

HOW MUCH DO YOU KNOW? (5 mins)

Give them the following pairs of statements. Ask them to vote on which of the pair is true.

1. Most pre-teens go through a 'homosexual phase' in which they develop crushes on people of the same sex, but this is a normal stage which passes / Not many pre-teens go through a 'homosexual phase' in which they develop crushes on people of the same sex; if they do, this is a sign that they are turning gay.

2. Some people may be born with a tendency towards homosexuality, but for most it seems to be acquired from their environment / Homosexuality is something you are born with, and there's nothing anybody can do about it.

3. When a homosexual becomes a Christian, God sometimes removes the sexual orientation, but not always / When a homosexual becomes a Christian, there is total liberty from the previous sexual orientation

In each case, the first statement is generally accepted to be the correct one. When you give the answers, use the opportunity to enlarge on the points a little and supply more information. For good background reading and a solid biblical approach, contact True Freedom Trust, PO Box 3, Upton, Wirral, Merseyside L49 6NY. Unless you already know a lot about it, you will have to do some research in order to teach this subject responsibly.

THERE OUGHT TO BE A LAW (15–20 mins)

Divide into small groups. Hand out copies of the sheet opposite which contains statements (opinions regularly voiced by different people) and a list of Bible passages.

Ask them to look at each statement in turn. What does it say that's right from a biblical point of view? What does it say that's wrong? After deciding that, ask them to construct their own ideal statement of a biblical approach to homosexuality and homosexuals. Allow them about 12 minutes and then get their feedback and encourage discussion.

QUESTION TIME (OPTIONAL)

Appoint a Question Time-type panel to try to answer questions like those below. Allow plenty of interaction from the audience in order to have a lively debate. The practice it gives will help the young people argue biblically about some of the central issues:

- What should you do if a friend confides in you that he or she is homosexual?
- What should the laws governing gays be?
- Is it really fair to expect people to go without sexual experience for a lifetime?
- What should happen to a church member who's found to be cruising around gay bars?

THERE OUGHT TO BE A LAW!

Look at each of the three statements below in turn. What does it say that's right from a biblical point of view? What does it say that's wrong? After deciding that, construct your own ideal statement of a biblical approach to homosexuality and homosexuals.

1) 'What should Christians do about homosexuality? I'll tell you. They should condemn it utterly and entirely as an abomination and something evil. God's pattern for human sexuality is one man and one woman in marriage, and anybody who veers off into depravity needs to be wholeheartedly shunned until they give up their wickedness. Homosexual conduct should be punished by law and persistent offenders should be hospitalised. That would stop them.'

Right . . . .
. . . .
. . . .

Wrong . . . .
. . . .
. . . .

2) 'Homosexual love can be as pure, committed and noble as heterosexual love. People of a homosexual orientation didn't ask to be that way; it was the sexuality they were given by a loving Creator God who doesn't make mistakes. We need to confront our own fear and rejection of homosexuals and reach out to them as respected equals. We cannot ask people to deny their own basic nature. Christian love demands that we affirm and accept them.'

Right . . . .
. . . .
. . . .

Wrong . . . .
. . . .
. . . .

3) 'The Bible never condemns a homosexual nature – just homosexual practice. And so we can love and accept homosexuals as long as they are willing to remain chaste and celibate. We should also respect the right of non-Christians in society to live a homosexual lifestyle, as long as they are doing no harm to others. We must challenge homosexual Christians to believe that God will deliver them from their condition, and if this hasn't happened after a year or so we must rebuke them for their lack of faith.'

Right . . . .
. . . .
. . . .

Wrong . . . .
. . . .
. . . .

Bible passages: Leviticus 18:22; Romans 1:18–27; 1 Corinthians 6:9–11; Galatians 6:1–2; 2 Timothy 2:24–26.

Our own ideal statement of a biblical approach to homosexuality and homosexuals:

. . . .
. . . .
. . . .
. . . .
. . . .

PARENTS

BEFORE THE EVENT...

Ask four group members to be prepared to act out a role-play situation during the meeting. They will be members of the same (Christian) family, sitting at the tea table when the 15-year-old daughter casually mentions that she is going out bowling with the youth club and will need £5 and a lift home at 10:30pm. She had (sort of) mentioned it a week ago, but hadn't provided any details. The mother is upset because she was counting on the daughter's help in the garden that evening. The father was planning to watch a big football match on TV and it won't be over until 10:45. The 14-year-old brother is upset because he's never allowed out until 10:30 and he hasn't been given any pocket money for three weeks. The father reminds him that his pocket money was stopped because he hadn't been doing his homework. The son asks if the daughter has done her homework...she hasn't. From this point the argument can go any way the actors like.

Ask them not to rehearse it together beforehand – it has to be spontaneous, spur-of-the-moment stuff – but to think through what it would be natural to say and do in that situation. They shouldn't decide beforehand whether the argument just gets worse or whether they patch it all up... but wait to see how it goes on the night.

NICEST FAMILY MEMBER AWARD (10 mins)

Hand out paper and pens to everyone. Tell them this is a quest to find the star son or daughter of the week. Then give them these instructions:
● Give yourself three points if you washed the dishes this week
● Lose two points if you never wash the dishes
● Gain one point if you spoke to your parents for more than two minutes today
● Lose one point if your bedroom is untidy at this moment
● Gain five points if you haven't argued with your parents all week
● Lose two points for each time you have had an argument in the last two days
● If you have done something unexpectedly nice for your parents this week, add four points

● If your parents have done something unexpectedly nice for you, add two points
● If you forgot to say 'thank you', lose those points again
● If you criticised your parents to your friends, lose three points
● If your parents embarrassed you in front of someone else, gain three points
● If you sulked as a result, lose them again
(You may wish to alter some instructions or add more of your own – that's fine.) Let them add up their scores, and give a suitable small award to the winner.

Then say: 'Parents and children often find it difficult to live together. Even in the most peaceful households, adults and teenagers don't always see eye to eye. Clearly it's always been like that. A large part of Proverbs – a book written for the instruction of young people – talks at length about parents. Even in those days parents could be a problem.'

So what are the difficulties? And what has the Bible to say that helps us?

WHY PARENTS ARE WEIRD (15 mins)

Hand out photocopies of the sheet opposite. The aim is to get the group to discuss the major hassles they have with their own parents. The discussion questions should be used to launch them into talking about it. Having got them to talk about their own gripes and complaints, try to get them to see both sides of the picture. Why are parents the way they are? Have they got good reasons for feeling and acting as they do? Do teenagers ever contribute to their own problems?

JUST A NORMAL FAMILY? (15 mins)

Homer Simpson warns his cartoon kids, 'Remember, as far as anyone knows, we're just a normal family.' But normal families can be just as riotous as the Simpsons. Get four people to act out the family situation you have previously prepared.

Allow the scene to run a fair while so that each character's point of view is clearly expressed, but kill it before the actors run out of ideas. Then divide the group into four. Ask each small group to focus on one of the characters, and to discuss together:
● What was reasonable and what was unreasonable in this character's point of view?
● What did this character do to make the situation worse than it needed to be?
● What did this character do to improve the situation and help bring understanding?
● What could this character have done which would have produced a better result quicker?
● If you had one piece of advice for this character, what would it be?

Sum up: Often in family disputes, right and

wrong are hard to sort out. Nobody is right all the time, and families don't work unless there is forgiveness, reconciliation and a willingness to admit when we're wrong. It's time to look at what God says.

WHAT GOD THINKS ABOUT YOUR PARENTS (10 mins)

In the four small groups, read Ephesians 6: 1–4, Colossians 3:20–21 and Proverbs 4:1–7. Then get each group to write down their conclusions, based on these verses, concerning the following:
● What parents are for
● What parents should do for children
● How children should react to their parents
● What happens if this all takes place properly?
● What happens if you don't get it right?

WHAT WOULD YOU DO IF... (10 mins)

Now give the four small groups a number of 'What would you do if...' problems to solve. Read out each problem, give them two minutes to talk about it, then award one point for the funniest answer, one for the strangest answer, three for the most practical answer, and five for the most biblical answer. (Obviously, if an answer is brilliantly funny, practical, strange and biblical, it scoops the pool!

'What would you do if...'
● '...you came home from school and your mum had helpfully wallpapered your bedroom a truly dreadful colour, expecting you to like it?'
● '...your dad suddenly took a violent dislike to your boyfriend and forbade you to see him again?'
● '...you met your mum in the street while you were with your friends, and she started telling that embarrassing story about you when you were three years old?'
● '...all your friends were going on this really exciting youth group trip to Romania, when your parents decide they can't afford it, and anyway you're too young?'

What this exercise is trying to do is to give the group practice in thinking through how they should apply the Bible's perspectives on parents and children to their own family life.

PARENT PRAYER (5 mins)

End by praying together. Ask the group to think in silence about their parents – the things they love and admire, and the things that really irritate. Pray together that God will bless them, and help us to be more effective in bringing the best out of them, and playing our role in the family in the way that God intended. Make it clear that you're available to help if anybody would like a personal chat about some of these issues.

Why Parents are WEIRD

Answer the Questions below:

1 How many ways can you think of that parents embarrass young people? List them...

2 What on earth makes them do these things?

3. Which phrases do parents use again & again, like a stuck record?

4. Why Do They keep Saying These Things?

5 If you could give parents three bits of advice, what would they be?

6 Which are the main ways in which parents are totally unfair to young people? Why?

7. What are the most common things teenagers do that make parents see red? Why?

8 Complete this sentence: 'If I ever become a parent I will never...

SECTION 2

WHO IS JESUS?

These half-dozen meeting outlines do not paint the full picture of who Jesus was – how could they? But I do believe they portray a creative and powerful presentation of aspects of Jesus' character and works which are often neglected. The central themes of Christ's death and resurrection are covered in this book's predecessor, 40 Ready-To-Use Meeting Guides (Kingsway),and you may like to add those to these six. Either way, with careful and prayerful preparation, these meetings will help provide a powerful introduction to the God Man Jesus Christ!

1. JESUS THE RADICAL
Considers the question: 'What does it mean to be a radical like Jesus?'

2. JESUS THE SERVANT KING
We serve Christ as we serve others. Includes an act of service by you the youth leaders/workers!

3. JESUS THE COMPASSIONATE
Explores how Jesus showed compassion, and how your group can be motivated to get involved in compassionate action.

4. JESUS THE POWER WORKER
Considers the awesome power and authority of Christ over nature, sickness and evil, and his compassion for the poor and weak.

5. JESUS THE STORY-TELLER
Focuses on the parable of the unfruitful fig tree which warns of the consequences of a lack of spiritual growth.

6. JESUS THE VINE
Focuses on the parabolic title of 'Jesus the Vine' and its meaning – we need to stay connected to Jesus in order to bear fruit.

JESUS THE RADICAL

JAMMY DODGERS (5 mins)

Get everyone to line up into two teams of equal size for this crazy crowdbreaker. Each team has to carry cotton wool balls from one end of the room to the other and drop them into a bucket. They may, however, only be carried on the nose! The game starts when you simultaneously open two pots of jam. Team members rush to the jam, stick their noses in, then rush to the cotton wool balls. They carry them down the room and into their team bucket. They cannot use their hands to remove the cotton wool. Vigorous head shaking and nodding should be enough to get the ball off the nose and into the bucket.

Allow the game to run for about three minutes. Be sure to have a Polaroid or VCR to record the mayhem and then show the pictures.

Use this game to introduce the theme of 'radical or ridiculous'.

RADICAL OR RIDICULOUS (10–15 mins)

Hand out pens and copies of the worksheet opposite to every member of your group. Ask them to complete the questionnaire, then get some feedback. Allow people to discuss and debate their different opinions on what is radical and what is ridiculous. Make the point that we don't all agree on what makes something radical. Radical actions can often seem ridiculous and attract ridicule or even opposition.

RADICAL PEOPLE (20 mins)

Read out these three potted histories of people considered ridiculous by many people in their time, but who are now revered as radicals. Ask the group to identify why some ridiculed them during their campaign to change aspects of the society they lived in.

● **Sarah Mapp Douglass** (1806–1882) and **Lucretia Mott** (1793–1850) were school-teachers, one black and one white. With others, they set up the Female Anti-Slavery Society in 1833. They were determined to stand up and speak out, in spite of their meetings being attacked by racist mobs. Slavery was finally abolished in America in 1865.

● **Emmeline Pankhurst** (1858–1928) set up the Women's Social and Political Union in 1903. Within four years there were 3,000 branches throughout the UK and her paper, *Votes For Women*, sold 40,000 copies a week. The campaign for the right of women as well as men to have the vote resulted in many suffragettes being imprisoned. Inside prison many women went on hunger strike and suffered from forced feeding. Pankhurst was sent to Holloway prison a dozen times.

● **Anthony Ashley Cooper**, Lord Shaftesbury (1801–1885) was a politician and social reformer who had a deep love for the poor. He campaigned tirelessly to limit factory hours, to stop the use of boys as chimney sweeps and children in coal mines, and to develop education for all. Britain was changed as a result of his lifelong work which included the founding of several organisations and charities.

Hand out Bibles, paper and pens and in small groups of two or three ask your young people to list which aspects of the radical message and lifestyle of Jesus were considered ridiculous by some of the people at the time. If your young people know their Bibles and the life of Christ well, leave them to it, however if they need some prompting put the list of scripture passages below onto an OHP or whiteboard to give them some prompts (this is not a comprehensive list of examples of Jesus' radical words or deeds). Allow up to 10 minutes then get feedback.

Matthew 8:1–4; 9:9–13
attitude towards social outcasts – touching and healing leper, calling of Matthew

Matthew 12:1–14
breaks empty religious taboos – Lord of the Sabbath

Matthew 16:13–17; 26:63–64
claims to be Son of God, – Jesus and Peter, before Chief Priest

Mark 5:1–20
power to heal, attitude to outcasts – healing of demon-possessed man

Luke 6:27–36
love your enemies

Luke 7:36–50
accepts extravagant gift from sinful woman – anointed by perfume

Luke 12:13–21
use of stories, attitude to money – parable of the rich fool

Luke 12:49–52
not peace but division – his message will divide families

Luke 18:18–30
cost of becoming a follower – rich young ruler

John 2:13–17
righteous anger – clears the temple

John 4:1–26
attitude towards women and foreigners – talks with Samaritan woman

John 8:1–11
doesn't condemn – woman caught in adultery

John 12:12–16
Christ's humility – he enters Jerusalem on a young donkey

MODERN-DAY RADICALS (15 mins)

Keep the young people in their small groups and ask them to consider the following questions. Allow them a few minutes to come up with an answer to the first, then get feedback and discussion. Do the same with the other two questions. Encourage an openness to consider unlikely suggestions, this exercise is designed to get them thinking about applying Jesus' radical lifestyle to themselves today.

1) If Jesus was on the earth today, aged 16 and living in our town, what sort of radical lifestyle / behaviour would he adopt and call others to follow?

2) What aspects of his radical lifestyle would offend people?

3) Which groups of people would find Jesus particularly radical or ridiculous?

Radical, Ridiculous or both?

Tick the box beside each statement depending on whether the idea is, in your opinion, radical, ridiculous or both.

Radical	Ridiculous	Both	
☐	☐	☐	Eating a raw onion
☐	☐	☐	Having a poisonous snake as a pet
☐	☐	☐	Buying your clothes from a charity shop
☐	☐	☐	Witnessing about Jesus to your friends
☐	☐	☐	Telling your girl/boy friend that they have bad breath
☐	☐	☐	Telling someone you like to listen to Boyzone
☐	☐	☐	Reading a Bible at school in the lunch break
☐	☐	☐	Pouring Coca Cola over your corn flakes
☐	☐	☐	Joining a political party or pressure/campaigning group
☐	☐	☐	Making friends with someone who is unpopular
☐	☐	☐	Telling your mum that her cooking is awful
☐	☐	☐	Admitting your homework is late because you watched TV last night
☐	☐	☐	Going on a blind date

JESUS THE SERVANT KING

MEETING AIM: The central and most important component in this meeting is an act of service by the youth leaders to the young people. From this deed, which should mirror your ongoing commitment to them, you should apply the theme of service – how we serve Christ as we serve others and that there is joy in service. If you follow this suggested outline – preparing and serving a three-course meal for your group – this will require considerable preparation and, depending on the size of your group, could be expensive! However, if you can manage this I recommend you go the extra mile as the teaching theme will be considerably reinforced through it. Reading the chapters on 'submission' and 'service' in Richard Foster's excellent *Celebration of Discipline*, published by Hodder & Stoughton, will help your preparation.

FANTASY FIVE MINUTES (10 mins)

Tell the group that they are going to be able to fantasise about their dream place to visit. Ask them to imagine where in the world they would like to be instantly whisked to for a fortnight. Hand out some exotic holiday brochures that you have collected from a travel agent's, plus any visitor's guides to far-away destinations or foreign capitals you can find. Alternatively suggest a few ideas such as Bali, Sydney, Rio de Janeiro, New York, Cape Town, Hong Kong, Moscow or Delhi. Allow them 30 seconds' thinking time and then ask them to call out their destinations. Make a list on an OHP or whiteboard, asking each person to briefly explain their choice.

Repeat this exercise, but this time offer the group their choice of time as well as place to visit between 3000BC and AD3000. You could suggest a few ideas, such as Hastings in 1066 to watch the battle, 1776 in America when they declared independence.

Now ask the group why Jesus Christ voluntarily obeyed his Father, who chose for him to be born as a human being into a poor family with a humble trade living in an obscure region of a downtrodden country under occupation from a foreign force 2,000 years ago. God could have chosen a more comfortable time and place for his Son to be born – so why then and there? Discuss. (As an example of servanthood, because God had a special affection for the poor, because the time period had a common language [Greek] in a large geographical area of Europe, the Middle East, North Africa and parts of Asia and a good road system which helped the message Jesus brought to spread more easily.)

THE PROMISED ONE (5 mins)

For many centuries the Jewish nation had been looking forward to the arrival of the Messiah, the promised one. The Old Testament contains many references to the sort of person the Messiah would be. Ask individuals to look up one of the verses below and then in turn read them out. Alternatively, if this is inappropriate for your group, write down the verses on an OHP acetate or whiteboard.

Read these Old Testament references to build up the servant aspect of the sort of person God promised to send.
- Isaiah 42:1–4; 49:1–7; 50:4–9; 52:13–53:12
- Ezekiel 34:23–24; 37:24–25
- Zechariah 3:8

Also refer to Matthew 12:17-21, which shows how Jesus fulfilled one of these predictions that God would choose to send a servant, and Matthew 20:20–28, where Jesus describes himself as a servant.

The most radical social teaching of Jesus was his total reversal of the contemporary notion of greatness. Leadership is found in becoming the servant of all…It is impossible to overstate the revolutionary character of Jesus' life and teaching at this point. He did away with all the claims to privileged position and status. It called into being a whole new order of leadership…He flatly told his disciples, "If any one would be first, he must be last of all and servant of all" (Mark 9:35).

From *Celebration of Discipline* by Richard Foster (Hodder & Stoughton)

MODERN-DAY FOOT-WASHING (50–80 mins)

Depending on the size of your group and your meeting location prepare, cook and serve a three-course meal for everyone. Maybe you can get in a little extra help to make this possible, but it is very important that the regular group leaders do most of the work! Leave the washing up till the end of the meeting – and use the post-meal and meeting time to build further on relationships. Refuse any kind offers to do the washing up from the young people. Tonight is the night when the leaders serve the young people – even more than usual.

The actual content of the meal is up to you. Try to make it something the young people will enjoy. One option to cut down on preparation time beforehand and to allow the leaders to spend some quality time during the meal instead of rushing around clearing plates and serving the next course, is to make it more of a 'cheese and nibbles buffet'. Have lots of different crisps, savoury biscuits, breadsticks, satay sticks, cheeses, and sliced carrot, celery and cucumber with various dips. Keep topping up the bowls and introduce new flavours. Maybe follow this up with a selection of mini-size chocolate bars with a coffee. Whatever style of meal you opt for, the lead-

ers should be serving the young people.

Conclude the meal with a reading of John 13:1–17. Explain that you have performed a modern version of foot-washing by preparing and serving the meal to them. Use this opportunity to briefly unpack the reasons why the leaders run the youth club/group. Without becoming over-intense, this is an ideal opportunity for you to tell the group that you care about them, want the best for them, long to see them grow and develop into balanced people who love God, have a healthy self-image, care about and serve other people and God's world, etc. Often young people don't really stop and think through why people deal with the hassle of running a youth club/group. However, be careful not to labour these points. Be humble; don't let this become an 'aren't we wonderful' speech! Make sure you say that ultimately you are involved and serve because of what God has done for you and that you are following Christ's example. He was born into poverty, and showed his solidarity with the poor by getting alongside people and helping them in practical and spiritual ways. He demonstrated a new form of leadership, where authority is earned not taken, and where the leader serves instead of lording it over others.

In small groups ask the young people to briefly read through the story from John 13 and then answer these two questions:

1. What did Jesus mean in verse 17 about being blessed? (service is enriching, it is obeying Christ, it is a part of discipleship, it is a spiritual discipline)

2) In the Middle East where people walked on dusty roads wearing open sandals, foot-washing was an important regular hygienic necessity. If you had a servant or slave they would normally do this for you. What modern-day equivalent jobs, tasks or acts of voluntary service compare to foot-washing 2,000 years ago?

All the youth workers should then take bowls of water and wash and dry the feet of the group. What does servant leadership mean?

WHO TO SERVE (5 mins)

Hand out copies of the sheet opposite, or alternatively photocopy the image onto a (photocopiable) OHP acetate and project onto the wall or a screen. Get the group to consider and discuss the question 'Who is it easier to serve and why?' (eg tramp has more obvious need but harder to love; woman has less obvious need but looks friendlier…).

SERVICE WITH A SMILE (10+ mins)

Get your group to brainstorm ways they could get involved in serving others. Ideally, beforehand you should check out a couple of local opportunities which you could suggest and add to the list if they are struggling to think of any ideas, eg serving in a charity shop, offering hospitality, carrying out an errand, helping out in a homeless shelter or late night soup run. Having made a long list, go back through the ideas and identify together one which they as individuals could do (or do more of). This can be as simple and practical as offering to do the washing up at home!

Also ask the group to identify something they could attempt together. Spend some time thinking through the practical implications and obstacles which stand in the way of achieving this group service task. Challenge the group to consider getting involved and help them in the planning process. However, it needs to be their decision – don't try to force or persuade them into service. If they decide that none of the ideas will work, or that they are not prepared to commit themselves to making it work, let it drop.

Details of short-term mission opportunities are given below. Although this can involve a lot of work and planning they are well worth facilitating as the young people will be changed for the better by the experience.

SHORT-TERM SERVICE OPPORTUNITIES OPTIONS
The whys and wherefores of sending your young people away.

Each year several thousand young British Christians get involved in short-term mission or service projects. These young people want to make a difference – and the process of serving others makes a difference to them too!

'Short-term mission projects, properly executed and led, are the best opportunity in youth ministry for the discipling and development of youth as leaders and as growing people,' according to Paul Borthwick, writing in *Nurturing Young Disciples* (Marshall Pickering). Borthwick has had over 20 years of intense involvement in sending youth and adults on short-term mission teams.

'Youth teams have built houses, painted buildings, dug wells, led Bible Clubs, preached at churches, led in evangelistic campaigns and any number of other ministries. Many parents have commented, "We sent our teenager off as an immature youth and received him back as a growing young adult."'

Fellow American Tony Campolo is just as positive. Well known as an author, speaker and professor-at-large for Eastern College, he is an ardent supporter of short-term service and has helped develop its use in projects he is involved with. Also writing in *Nurturing Young Disciples* he points out that 'as short-term workers struggle to help others they do more than they are able to realise at the time. In helping others…even in the midst of social insanity, they discover community and identity. As they reflect on what has happened they realise and renew their calling. They experience Jesus telling them who they are.'

Each year Christian Vocations (CV) produces an updated brochure of the wide range of short-term service and mission opportunities available through Christian organisations.

Soapbox Expeditions is just one of many other similar organisations listed in CV's *Short-Term Directory* which send young people abroad on short projects. Work includes building and maintenance work, health education, medical care, evangelism and humanitarian aid projects.

Unfortunately many projects do not accept volunteers who are younger teens. However, there are some schemes available, although very few involve overseas service opportunities.

The Short-Term Service Directory lists short-term opportunities. Write for more details and an order form to: CV, Holloway Street West, Lower Gornal, Dudley, West Midlands DY3 2DZ.

Who is it easier to serve and why?

JESUS THE COMPASSIONATE

MEETING AIM: To explore how Jesus showed compassion, and how your group can be motivated to get involved in compassionate action.

COMPASSION REACTION

Before the meeting photocopy onto acetate (you need special photocopiable acetate sheets) the quotes opposite. Then use an OHP to project the quotes onto a screen or wall as people enter the room where you hold your meeting. It would be good to have music playing in the background – if you can get hold of it *Do They Know It's Christmas?* from the Live Aid concert.

NEWSPAPER SEARCH (15 mins)

Hand out copies of both local and national papers. Divide the group into sub-groups and ask them to look through the newspaper, picking out stories which fall into the following categories:

● situations that are hard for us to change, eg earthquakes;
● things that are relatively easy to change, eg attitudes;
● situations that can be changed if people worked together, eg poverty;
● things that individuals can change eg, selfishness.

Get the group to analyse how the papers have reported on the story sympathetically, factually and so on. Ask them to think how reading the article made them feel – whether they felt powerless, guilty or just disinterested.

Get each group to do a two-minute presentation from the perspective of someone affected by the story. For example, if it's a story about bullying, what is it like to be the parent of someone who is being bullied?

REAL LIFE (15 mins)

Invite someone – possibly from your church – who is involved in compassionate work or who has experienced the compassion of others, to come in and tell their story. People involved in nursing, mission and social work often have good stories to tell about compassion.

BACKGROUND

Increasingly we're confronted with images of suffering on TV. Those images often demonstrate the lack of compassion or simple human kindness in society. Compassion has been defined as 'the willingness to have your personal agenda shaped, or changed, by the needs of others'.

How much compassion we demonstrate is often linked to the value we give people. When we understand how much people are worth – that God created us all unique and

equal – we're more likely to show compassion. Most people involved in compassionate work such as social work, youth work and missionary work are motivated by the value they place on people.

Many of us struggle to know what to do when we encounter large-scale suffering like famine and homelessness. Often guilt, feelings of failure and the enormousness of the problem stop us getting involved.

It's been said that many of us suffer from compassion fatigue.

But there are many times when we can show compassion every day by doing 'simple acts of kindness and love'. Too often we don't do them because we're too busy with our own lives. Basically, we're too selfish to care.

Encourage your group to look out for opportunities to show compassion to the people around them – the homeless, the elderly, and others who are marginalised.

BIBLE COMPASSION (10–15 mins)

Throughout the New Testament there are many stories of Jesus being compassionate towards the people around him. Hand out Bibles/Gospels and ask the young people, in small groups, to find two examples of Jesus' compassion.

Allow about five minutes for searching and then have feedback. Ask the groups to explain why they chose their examples and what it illustrates about Jesus' compassionate nature. For example: feeding of the 5,000 (Matthew 14:13–21) – Jesus has just heard that John the Baptist, his cousin, had been beheaded. Knowing the implications of this action for his own life, he needs some space away to think and pray. He decides to get away from the crowds by taking a boat trip across the lake. Unfortunately, the crowds follow him by foot, so when Jesus arrives, they're already waiting for him.

Instead of turning the boat around and going back to the other side of the lake, Jesus puts his need for solitude on hold and responds by showing them compassion. He shows his concern practically by healing the sick, teaching them about the kingdom, and being concerned about their lack of food.

Say: 'Some people say that the Bible is basically a record of the greatest story of compassion the world has ever known; that God looked down on his creation, saw the position humankind had got into, and made the ultimate sacrifice to rectify the situation.'

WHAT IF? (20 mins)

Get your group to discuss how they would react in the following situation. It's 1 am. You're tired. You've just finished work in a city

about 50 miles from home. The road home takes you through the countryside and a dense forest. Halfway home you pass a car that's stopped on the brow of a hill. As you drive past, you notice the car has a puncture. Because it's so late, you know there'll be very little traffic on the road.

What do you do? Ignore the situation and drive on, or stop to help? What are the implications of doing nothing or stopping to help?

The above situation actually happened. The driver drove past, then turned back to help. In the car were two women and three children under ten. They were all very frightened. They'd broken down seven hours earlier. No one had stopped to help, or even inform the police of their predicament.

Say: 'This is just a small example of everyday compassion. History is littered with stories of people who've performed amazing acts of heroic compassion. But they didn't start by doing the big potentially life-threatening stuff. They started small, where they were.'

Refer to Jesus' parable of the Good Samaritan (Luke 10:25–37). In Jewish society, Samaritans were looked down upon by everyone – especially the religious leaders. They were considered to be the lowest of the low. In this parable, Jesus depicts the Samaritan as the hero. Verses 33–35 express the Samaritan taking much trouble to ensure the well-being of the victim. First he goes to where the victim is, dresses his wounds, puts him on his donkey, takes him to an inn where he takes care of him, and then pays the innkeeper to look after him. The Samaritan really goes the 'extra mile' to help out someone he doesn't even know, and who has probably been prejudiced against Samaritans.

Say: 'Showing compassion is like most things in the Christian life – it's about taking small steps and God meeting you where you are at. The Bible talks about Jesus doing amazing things like bringing people back to life. Then it goes on to say that we'll do 'greater things' than he did. We might think: Well, it was easy for Jesus because he was the Son of God and he knew exactly what to do. For many of us, the fear of getting it wrong or previous bad experience when our intentions were misunderstood stops us from getting involved.

'Christians have been given a gospel that's good news to the poor, gives sight to the blind, sets prisoners free and releases the oppressed.'

Close by asking your group to pray for each other for God-given opportunities to show compassion to others.

I SEE PEOPLE SUFFERING AND IT MAKES ME SAD.

MOTHER TERESA

IF YOU THINK YOU'RE TOO SMALL TO MAKE A DIFFERENCE, YOU'VE OBVIOUSLY NEVER BEEN IN BED WITH A MOSQUITO.

ANITA RODDICK

TO SAY WE HAVE COMPASSION FATIGUE IS TO SAY WE HAVE LOVE FATIGUE.

BILLY CONNOLLY

THERE'S A WORLD OUTSIDE YOUR WINDOW AND IT'S A WORLD OF DREAD AND FEAR,
WHERE THE ONLY WATER FLOWING IS THE BITTER STING OF TEARS.
AND THE CHRISTMAS BELLS THAT RING THERE ARE THE CLANGING CHIMES OF DOOM,
SO TONIGHT THANK GOD IT'S THEM INSTEAD OF YOU.

'DO THEY KNOW IT'S CHRISTMAS?'

JESUS THE POWER WORKER

MEETING AIM: To teach on the power and authority of Christ over nature, sickness and evil; to show that Jesus had compassion and love for people and used his power to help people and as a sign of his ultimate authority and identity. This meeting plan requires the young people to use considerable imagination. Even if your group finds the first role-play reading difficult, persevere. The reward for doing so could be considerable, as the meeting concludes with an opportunity to enter into God's family.

Introduce this session by explaining that the theme is the word 'power', which means 'to have control, authority or influence over things or people'.

POWER QUIZ (8 mins)
Hand out pens and photocopies of the quiz sheet opposite or photocopy it onto an OHP acetate. Award an appropriate prize for the person or small group who can successfully fill in the blanks first, or those who get most right after five minutes.
ANSWERS:
1) tools, 2) point, 3) boat, 4) to your elbow, 5) station or plant, 6) rangers, 7) house, 8) breaker, 9) dressing, 10) cut.

POWERFUL PEOPLE (5 mins)
The word 'power' means 'to have control, authority or influence over things or people'. Ask the group to call out people or groups of people who are powerful (Prime Minister, owner of a national newspaper, chairman of a multi-national company, headteacher, class bully etc). Make a list on an OHP or white board.

If you are a relative or friend of a powerful person, that can give you some influence too. Ask the group to think of an influential or powerful person whom they benefit from knowing because it gives them influence. Make a second list. Then explain that you will come back to this list later...

POWER CLIPS (10 mins)
Gather together two or three short film clips to show on a video at some point during the meeting (probably best after the first of the three role-play readings which come next). These short clips should be from disaster movies of volcanoes exploding, tornadoes ripping up houses, floods washing away people, fires destroying tower blocks, etc. This should highlight the power of nature and the frailty of humans when faced with its raw power.

ROLE-PLAY READINGS (30 mins)
Use this exercise to give the group a fresh understanding of and insight into a Bible story. Assign different group members to become the following people from these Bible stories from *The Message*.* Explain that as you read the verses, they should try to imagine how they (their character) would have felt. Ask them to close their eyes and imagine the sights, sounds and even smells that the story conjures up!

Read the passage through slowly and pause for 15 seconds where you see this symbol #. Have a watch or stopwatch with you so you can time a full 15-seconds pause. This will allow for thinking and feeling time as they enter into their roles. Also read out the guide notes in brackets.

At the completion of each story ask each person/character in turn to say how they felt at the different points of the story. This can be a very powerful way of reading and experiencing Scripture, although some people find it hard to concentrate. Hopefully, most of the group will, by the second or third role-play reading, see the value of the exercise and be able to empathise with their character and experience the story in a fresh way.

Matthew 8:23–27
Characters: Jesus, 12 disciples.
Set the scene by saying: 'The story centres around a boat trip. Remember that several of the disciples are hardy fishermen and used to travelling and working in boats on a rough sea.'

Then he [that is Jesus] got in the boat, his disciples with him. #
The next thing they knew, they were in a severe storm [imagine what that was like in a wooden fishing boat, with high wind, rain and waves all around] #
Waves were crashing into the boat #
and he [that is Jesus] was sound asleep! #
They roused him #
pleading, 'Master, save us! We're going down!' #
Jesus reprimanded them. 'Why are you such cowards, such faint-hearts?' #
Then he stood up and told the winds to be silent, the sea to quiet down: 'Silence!' #
The sea became smooth as glass. #
The men rubbed their eyes, astonished, #
'What's going on here? Wind and sea come to heel at his command!' #

You may want to show the 'Power Clips' videos at this point to provide a short interlude in what could otherwise be quite a concentrated and intense exercise.

Luke 5:17–26
Characters: Jesus, Pharisees and religious teachers, paralysed man, paralysed man's friends, large crowd of onlookers.
Set the scene by saying: 'It was hot and sweaty and there were hoards of people all around. In other words, as far as the disciples were concerned, it was another typical day on the road with Jesus, and then something amazing happened...'

One day as Jesus was teaching, Pharisees and religious teachers were sitting around. #
They had come from nearly every village in Galilee and Judea, even as far away as Jerusalem, to be there. #
The healing power of God was on him. Some men arrived carrying a paraplegic on a stretcher. They were looking for a way to get into the house and set him before Jesus. #
When they couldn't find a way in because of the crowd, they went up on the roof, removed some tiles, and let him down in the middle of everyone, right in front of Jesus. #
Impressed by their bold belief, he said, 'Friend, I forgive your sins.' #
That set the religious scholars and the Pharisees buzzing. #
'Who does he think he is? That's blasphemous talk! God and only God can forgive sins.' #
Jesus knew exactly what they were thinking and said, 'Why all this gossipy whispering? Which is simpler: to say 'I forgive your sins,' or to say 'Get up and start walking'? #
Well just so it's clear that I'm the Son of Man and authorised to do either or both...' He spoke directly to the paraplegic: 'Get up. Take your bedroll and go home.' Without a moment's hesitation he did it – got up, [and] took his blanket, #
[the man] left for home, giving glory to God all the way. #
The people rubbed their eyes, incredulous – and then also gave glory to God. Awestruck, they said, 'We've never seen anything like that!' #

Luke 8:26–39
Characters: Jesus, demon-possessed man, disciples, pig herders, villagers from around Gerasene.
Set the scene by saying; 'It started off as just another day, but the disciples were in for a front-row spectacle of a power struggle the like of which they had never known before. At one moment it got very scary!'

[Jesus and his disciples] sailed on to the country of the Gerasenes, directly opposite Galilee. As he stepped out onto land, a madman from town met him, he was a victim of demons. He hadn't worn clothes for a long time, nor lived at home; he lived in the cemetery. #
When he saw Jesus he screamed, fell down before him, and bellowed, 'What business do you have messing with me? You're Jesus, Son of the High God, but don't give me a hard time!' The man said this because Jesus had started to

order the unclean spirit out of him. #

Time after time the demon threw the man into convulsions. #

He had been placed under constant guard and tied with chains and shackles, but crazed and driven wild by the demon, he would shatter the bonds. #

Jesus asked him, 'What is your name?'

'Mob. My name is Mob,' he said, because many demons afflicted him. And they begged Jesus desperately not to order them to the bottomless pit. #

A large herd of pigs was browsing and rooting on a nearby hill. The demons begged Jesus to order them into the pigs. He gave the order. It was even worse for the pigs than for the man. Crazed, they stampeded over a cliff into the lake and drowned. #

Those tending the pigs, scared to death, bolted and told their story in town and country. #

People went out to see what had happened. They came to Jesus and found the man from whom the demons had been sent, sitting there at Jesus' feet, wearing decent clothes and making sense. It was a holy moment, and for a short time they were more reverent than curious. #

Then those who had seen it happen told how the demoniac had been saved. #

Later a great many people from the Gerasene countryside got together and asked Jesus to leave – too much change, too fast and they were scared. #

So Jesus got back into the boat and set off. The man whom he had delivered from the demons asked to go with him, #

but he sent him back, saying, 'Go home and tell everything God did in you.' So he went back and preached all over town everything Jesus had done for him. #

Sum up by saying: 'These stories show how Jesus had amazing supernatural power. He had power over the forces of nature – like the waves and the wind – he had power over sickness and disease, he had power over evil forces and when he died and rose again he showed he had power over sin and death.'

POWERFUL PEOPLE II (7 mins)

Ask the young people to form small groups of two or three. Hand out paper and a pen to each group. Then remind them of the lists they made earlier. Ask each small group to select one person from the 'powerful people' list (but not an overtly negative character, eg a bully). Tell them they have to imagine how their life would change if that person was their father or mother. Get them to write down some of the consequences (eg money, able to attend posh film premieres, get to meet other powerful or famous people). Allow them three minutes and then get each group to feed back.

Conclude briefly by explaining how each person present can become a relative, literally a son or daughter, of the most powerful and influential being in the universe – God himself. We can become an adopted brother of Jesus.

Explain that Christians, when they pray, talk to Jesus, who then presents our prayers and petitions to God the Father on our behalf. Because of Jesus we can have access to God.

Invite anyone who does not have and enjoy this special relationship with God, but who wants it, to talk with you afterwards. Be prepared for surely the greatest privilege you can have as a Christian youth worker, to help lead a person into a relationship with Christ.

OPTIONAL EXTRA

Ask the group to discuss the statement 'There is power in powerlessness.' What examples from the life of Christ or the early church can they think of to suggest the statement is true?

Fill in the blank word(s) ...

1) power _____ electronic DIY implements

2) power _____ socket for connection of power to the mains

3) power _____ fast moving water-bourne craft

4) power _____ expression of encouragement or approval

5) power _____ building where electric power is generated

6) power _____ popular childrens TV programme featuring martial arts heroes

7) power _____ source of drive or influence

8) power _____ safety equipment for interrupting an electric current

9) power _____ wearing smart clothes to give an air of authority

10) power _____ temporary failure or withdrawal of power supply

JESUS THE STORY-TELLER

MEETING AIM: This session will inform and educate about how to interpret Jesus' parables and will focus on the parable of the unfruitful fig tree, which warns of the consequences of lack of repentance and spiritual growth.

Begin this session with one or both of these icebreaker games which introduce aspects of the theme of communication. This can then lead into the specific subject of parables, which Jesus used extensively as a method of communication.

DRAW IT! (5 mins)
Ask for two volunteers. Everyone else gets an A4 sheet of paper and a pencil. The volunteers take turns to describe objects and symbols which only they can see. From their description everyone else draws what they think is being described. The volunteers cannot use the name of the object, eg if they are describing a fork, they can't say, 'Draw a fork.' Instead they must describe its shape and approximate size, eg 'This object is a thin tube which becomes wider and flatter and stops with a rounded end. At the tube end it flattens into four long pointed little sticks which are parallel to each other.'

After each description ask the 'drawers' to hold up what they have drawn.

Get the volunteers to describe two objects or shapes each. The winner is the one whose description results in the most accurate drawings.

BOSSES AND SECRETARIES (10 mins)
Arrange players into couples, with each of the partners at opposite ends of the room. Use all the walls so that the players are spaced around the hall. One member of each couple (the boss) is given a prepared newspaper cutting (use six different messages of approximately the same length), while the other member (the secretary) has a piece of paper and a pencil. On the signal to start, the bosses begin dictating the contents of the newspaper cutting to the secretaries, who try to take it down. This is a difficult task with so many competing voices. The first couple with a complete correct message of dictation are the winners.

Variation: To make it more difficult, have the bosses sucking a lolly, standing on a chair on one leg.

Taken from: *Crowdbreakers* by Bob Moffett (Marshall Pickering) © 1983. Used with the permission of the author.

AD WATCH (5 mins)
Pre-record onto video some TV adverts which tell a story. Often it is impossible to tell what product is being promoted until towards the end of the ad. These 'story-telling' adverts engage interest and attention because the viewer wants to see how the 'story' will end. Having shown some adverts of this style, make the point that almost everyone enjoys a good story and that this week's meeting will focus on Jesus' ability to tell a good story, and on one story in particular that he told.

WHAT'S IT ALL ABOUT? (15 mins)
Ask the group to call out any facts they know about 'parables' and write down this information onto an OHP or whiteboard. Then complete any blanks in their knowledge from the points below:
● Parables were stories told by Jesus drawn from everyday life which people enjoyed listening to.
● Each parable contains one strong message/meaning/teaching point.
● Jesus' parables were unique. No Jewish rabbi before his lifetime used parables, although several did afterwards.
● Jesus' parables were often controversial and called for an answer or response on the spot. They often compelled the hearer to make a decision about Jesus and his mission.
● Many preachers allegorise Jesus' parables, giving meaning and significance to every character or thing in the story. This is a mistake and has led to some ridiculous and wrong teaching.
● Understanding a parable is helped by knowledge about the historical setting. For example, in the Parable of the Sower many consider the sower sowed his seed in a wasteful and carefree manner – sowing seeds (by mistake) on the path, in thorns or on stony ground. An understanding of how Palestinian farmers grew crops would reveal that sowing took place before ploughing. The sower intentionally sows on the path, since he intends to plough up the path, thorns and stubble. Nor is it surprising that some seed fell among rocks since the soil often barely covered the underlying limescale. So what seems to us today like bad farming was common practice.
● Understanding the meaning requires an examination of the context – the verses which immediately precede and follow the parable. This often reveals the true purpose Jesus had in telling the story.
● Jesus did not explain the meaning of the parable. He let his listeners work it out for themselves. However, on some occasions he gave the meaning privately to his disciples. End this section by asking the group to discuss these questions: 'Did everyone eventually come to the correct understanding of Jesus' parables? If not, does that mean it wasn't a very good method of communication?' Conclude by pointing them to Matthew 13:10–15, where Jesus explains to the disciples his reason for telling parables.

MODERN PARABLES (15–25 mins)
Divide everyone into small groups of two or three and hand out paper and pens. Then invite the groups to write a modern-day parable – a story with a meaning. The meaning or moral should be timeless (eg the fragile nature of life – you can't be sure of tomorrow), but set in a contemporary situation (eg a plane crash). Give the groups three minutes to select a moral, then seven minutes to write the story. Explain that the story should illustrate the moral, but may require some thought before it is obvious.

Once the stories have been written, get each group to read theirs out while the rest puzzle over its meaning, before being told if they are on track or not.

This feedback could get long and tiresome if you let it drag, so keep it moving along. You could choose to keep the meanings back until next week, or even never confirm them!

TREE TALE (15 mins)
If they are in season, buy a fresh fig and bring it along as a visual aid to help you retell the parable of the unfruitful fig tree from Luke 13:1–9. Read out this parable from a modern Bible translation, then ask the following questions (have them on an OHP or whiteboard) and ask the small groups to discuss and then feed back their answers.

1) Did Jesus say that the people killed by the Romans or crushed by the tower deserved what happened to them?

(No, Jesus made it clear that they were no more sinful than others, but he used the contemporary news stories to illustrate the fact that everyone would die and that those who died without receiving God's forgiveness would perish.)

2) What do you think Jesus meant by the parable he told about the fig tree (verses 6–9)?

(God demands that we be 'fruitful'. He allows some time to pass but if we fail to produce the goods within a reasonable period we can expect to be removed. In Palestine, vineyards were usually planted with fruit trees. Old Testament laws [Leviticus 19:23] allowed three years to go by before the fruit became ritually clean, therefore six years had elapsed since it was planted. The tree was barren. Since a fig tree absorbs a lot of nourishment from the soil, the surrounding vines were deprived of sustenance for no good. The gardener showed extraordinary patience and gave the tree one more year and every attention to promote fruit. At the end of another year it would be destroyed if it didn't fruit. Some scholars suggest that the gardener is a parallel of Jesus himself. When the limit granted by God is exhausted and time for repentance runs out, nothing can save it.)

3) What does this 'fruit' mean? What does God expect?

(This phrase is fairly common in the New Testament and usually means a visible product or quality of character and lifestyle. Christians 'bear fruit' when they obey God. Galatians talks of the 'fruit of the Holy Spirit', where God's presence in us makes us more like Christ and is characterised by qualities like joy, patience and self-control.)

GROWMORE (3 mins)

Hand out pens and copies of the sheet below. Explain that their completed sheets will not be seen by anyone else. Hand out an envelope to each person so that their sheet can be inserted into it then sealed. Make sure each person keeps their envelope as you go outside for the final part of this meeting.

PLANT A TREE (15 mins)

This may take a bit of organising but this exercise is well worth doing and will act as a memorable visual aid for years to come.

Get permission to plant a tree in the church grounds, or the grounds of a nearby property. Try to choose a fruit tree (eg apple, plum or even a fig!). Attempt to get the church to pay or maybe you have a youth work programme budget. Visit a local nursery or garden centre to buy a tree, consulting with the staff there about its size and eventual height. Have the tree, hole and soil to fill it ready, along with a couple of spades for a tree planting at the end of this meeting.

Begin by rereading the parable, then get each person to put their envelope into the hole. Emphasise the need to be fruitful now. Without being over-emotional or dramatic, simply explain that sadly one of this group may be dead 12 months from now – we don't know how long any of us have. It is important not to waste time, but to get on and 'bear fruit' in our lives and make them count.

Spend a moment in silence and then ask everyone to think of the areas of their life that they wrote down in which they would like to see 'fruit' grow and mature within the next year.

Conclude by praying for the group, asking Jesus to send his Holy Spirit to fill and empower each one and to work in them to bring about the fruit of the Spirit. Then read out Galatians 5:16–25.

As the tree grows it will give you an excellent opportunity regularly to remind your group of this week's lesson and follow up on spiritual progress in the months and even years to come.

In future years, as fruit grows and is picked from the tree, why not carefully pack the fruit in a padded envelope and post it on to individual group members who have maybe left, grown up or dropped away from church as a point of contact: 'Do you remember when we planted this tree x years ago…? It could prove a valuable and memorable visual aid to the group. And even if a vandal cuts it down or some other misfortune befalls it even this can be used as a powerful spiritual reminder of the original parable!

IN WHAT TWO AREAS OF YOUR LIFE WOULD YOU LIKE TO SEE 'FRUIT' GROW AND MATURE WITHIN THE NEXT YEAR?

JESUS THE VINE

MEETING AIM: To focus on one of the important parabolic titles Jesus gave himself; Jesus the Vine, and on its meaning (we need to stay connected to Jesus, and we need to bear fruit). We also look at what 'bearing fruit' could mean to Christian teens today.

BIBLE TAKE 1 (4 mins)

Photocopy the sheet opposite twice. This sheet contains three different versions of the same passage of Scripture, John 15:1–17. Cut them up and ask two confident readers to read alternate verses from version 1. Settle the group, then get your readers to read out loud to the rest of the group.

CHATEAU LE PONG (10 mins)

This is one of those icebreakers that your group will talk about for months afterwards – but have you got the bottle to go through with it? You will need the following props: two identical-size washing-up bowls, two bags of grapes which are identical in weight (preferably about 1lb/450g), two drying-up cloths/towels, two newspapers, a roll of kitchen paper, a sieve, two paper cups and a Pyrex jug which measures fluid ounces.

Ask for two volunteers who are wearing socks, and ask them to take their shoes and socks off. Meanwhile have a helper lay out the newspaper over the floor, put the washing-up bowls on the paper and put a bunch of grapes into each bowl. Explain to the volunteers that they have 20 seconds to trample on the grapes with their feet to create as much grape juice as they can. Explain that the loser will have to drink the winner's juice! Make sure that an assistant holds each bowl to prevent spillage while the volunteers energetically trample the grapes. After 20 seconds they stop and can dry their feet with kitchen roll and a towel. Sieve the fluid from the grape skins and pour into the measuring jug. Give the winner some wine gums, but keep your threat and encourage the loser to drink (at least some of) the winner's grape juice!

WORD ASSOCIATION (10 mins)

Ask for two volunteers to play a word association game. If you use the game above, volunteers may be thin on the ground unless you assure them that this is a harmless, no mess game. Explain that you will say a word and they must respond quickly with the first word that they associate with your word, eg bread – butter; drink – lemonade; night – sleep… While the first person is responding, ask the second to leave the room so they don't hear the words. That way they react off the cuff, as they haven't had time to prepare an answer. Then read out from the following list (the first few words to get them into the swing of it).

1. wash	2. hand
3. brush	4. friend
5. united	6. hug
7. attached	8. secure
9. connected	10. stay close
11. remain	12. join
13. couple	14. give

Debrief this exercise by reminding everyone of some of the words the volunteers said which link into the theme of staying close and connected – which is one of the main teaching points from the scripture reading. Explain that Christ wants his followers to be close and stay connected to him so that, like the vine, they will bear fruit.

BIBLE TAKE 2 (4 mins)

Read John 15:1–17 from version 2 to the group. Explain that this is from a paraphrase, not a direct translation of the Bible.

STAYING CONNECTED (15 mins)

Tell the group that you are going to conduct a demonstration to illustrate what Jesus meant by being connected to him.

Lay out nine paper cups on the floor or a table. 'Choose' a 'volunteer' who you have briefed beforehand. Now tell the group that the volunteer will leave the room while they choose a cup under which to place a grape. Say that you have such a good connection to the volunteer that he or she will be able to point out the cup that has the grape underneath when they re-enter the room.

Get the volunteer to leave the room. Ask the group to select a cup to place a grape under. When this is done invite the volunteer back into the room. Repeat the demonstration several times while the group tries to work out how the volunteer always manages to guess the right cup.

The trick is simple. Before the meeting starts recruit someone to be a 'volunteer', then tell them that you will sit facing the cups, with your legs visible to the volunteer. You indicate which cup was chosen by where you place your hand on your leg. They simply

need to see where on your leg your forefinger is resting (see diagram below).

When you finish your demonstration make the following point: The demonstration depended on the volunteer and me staying in communication – we needed to be connected. Christians need to stay connected to Jesus. We need to be aware of his messages and be willing to respond to them. Being connected to Jesus means listening to and obeying his words.

(Based on an activity in *Creative Bible Lessons in John* by Janice and Jay Ashcraft [Zondervan])

Ask:
● What are some specific things that you can do to 'remain in Jesus'?
● What sort of things might God do to 'prune' things from people's lives (verse 2)?
● What does Jesus mean by branches that are 'thrown away, wither…picked up, thrown in the fire and burned'?
● Verse 7 says, 'ask whatever you wish, and it will be given you.' What conditions do you think apply to that promise?

BIBLE TAKE 3 (10–15 mins)

Read John 15:1–17 a third time, but on this occasion dim or extinguish the lighting and light candles. Play some soft 'mood' instrumental music in the background. While reading John 15 from the third translation opposite, pause between each verse – the background music will help fill the silence and encourage a meditative and reflective atmosphere to develop. Reading this passage out a third time may seem over the top, but explain to your group that the idea is to really get under the skin of this passage of Scripture.

Having finished the reading, ask people to close their eyes and focus on the music and your words. Then read out verse 8 again and ask them to think about what Jesus meant by bearing fruit. Tell them to ask God's Holy Spirit to show them what fruit God wants to grow in their life. Allow a lengthy pause.

Then ask them to consider how 'bearing much fruit' will glorify God (verse 8), again allowing a pause for thinking while the music continues softly in the background. One or two may giggle or find it hard to concentrate. Gently encourage and correct them. Tell them to calm down, close their eyes and concentrate on listening to God through the Scripture and the questions they are considering.

Afterwards get some feedback from the group about what they got from the questions you posed.

Conclude by either praying a short prayer for them or, if you feel it appropriate, getting them into small groups to pray for each other.

BIBLE TAKE 1 – John 15:1-17

1 Jesus said to his disciples: I am the true vine, and my Father is the gardener.

2 He cuts away every branch of mine that doesn't produce fruit. But he trims clean every branch that does produce fruit, so that it will produce even more fruit.

3 You are already clean because of what I said to you.

4 Stay joined to me and I will stay joined to you. Just as a branch cannot bear fruit unless it stays joined to the vine, you cannot produce fruit unless you stay joined to me.

5 I am the vine, and you are the branches. If you stay joined to me, and I stay joined to you, then you will produce lots of fruit. But you cannot do anything without me.

6 If you don't stay joined to me, you will be thrown away. You will be like dry branches that are gathered up and burned in a fire.

7 Stay joined to me and let my teachings become part of you. Then you can pray for whatever you want, and your prayer will be answered.

8 When you become fruitful disciples of mine, my Father will be honoured.

9 I have loved you, just as my Father has loved me. So remain faithful to my love for you.

10 If you obey me, I will keep loving you, just as my Father keeps loving me because I have obeyed him.

11 I have told you this to make you as completely happy as I am.

12 Now I tell you to love each other, as I have loved you.

13 The greatest way to show love for friends is to die for them.

14 And you are my friends, if you obey me.

15 Servants don't know what their master is doing, and so I don't speak to you as my servants. I speak to you as my friends, and I have told you everything that my Father has told me.

16 You did not choose me. I chose you and sent you out to produce fruit, the kind of fruit that will last. Then my Father will give you whatever you ask for in my name.

17 So I command you to love each other.

BIBLE TAKE 2 – John 15:1-17

'I am the Real Vine and my Father is the Farmer. He cuts off every branch of me that doesn't bear grapes. And every branch that is grape-bearing he prunes back so it will bear even more. You are already pruned back by the message I have spoken.

'Live in me. Make your home in me just as I do in you. Live in the same way that a branch can't bear grapes by itself but only by being joined to the vine, you can't bear fruit unless you are joined with me.

'I am the Vine, you are the branches. When you're joined with me and I with you, the relation intimate and organic, the harvest is sure to be abundant. Separated, you can't produce a thing. Anyone who separates from me is deadwood, gathered up and burned on the bonfire. But if you make yourselves at home with me and my words are at home in you, you can be sure that whatever you ask you will be listened to and acted upon. This is how my Father shows who he is – when you produce grapes, when you mature as my disciples.

'I've loved you the way my Father has loved me. Make yourselves at home in my love. If you keep my commands, you'll remain intimately at home in my love. That's what I've done – kept my Father's commands and made myself at home in his love.

'I've told you these things for a purpose: that my joy might be your joy, and your joy wholly mature. This is my command: Love one another the way I loved you. This is the very best way to love. Put your life on the line for your friends. You are my friends when you do the things I command you. I'm no longer calling you servants because servants don't understand what their master is thinking and planning. No, I've named you friends because I've let you in on everything I've heard from the Father.

'You didn't choose me, remember; I chose you, and put you in the world to bear fruit, fruit that won't spoil. As fruit bearers, whatever you ask the Father in relation to me, he gives you.

'But remember the root command: Love one another.'

BIBLE TAKE 3 – John 15:1-17

'I am the true vine; my Father is the gardener. He cuts off every branch of mine that does not produce fruit. And he trims and cleans every branch that produces fruit so that it will produce even more fruit. You are already clean because of the words I have spoken to you. Remain in me, and I will remain in you. A branch cannot produce fruit alone but must remain in the vine. In the same way, you cannot produce fruit alone but must remain in me.

'I am the vine and you are the branches. If any remain in me and I remain in them, they produce much fruit. But without me they can do nothing. If any do not remain in me, they are like a branch that is thrown away and then dies. People pick up dead branches, throw them into the fire and burn them. If you remain in me and follow my teachings, you can ask anything you want, and it will be given to you. You should produce much fruit and show that you are my followers, which brings glory to my Father. I loved you as the Father loved me. Now remain in my love. I have obeyed my Father's commands, and I remain in his love. In the same way, if you obey my commands, you will remain in my love. I have told you these things so that you can have the same joy I have and so that your joy will be the fullest possible joy.

'This is my command: love each other as I have loved you. The greatest love a person can show is to die for his friends. You are my friends if you do what I command you. I no longer call you servants, because a servant does not know what his master is doing. But I call you friends, because I have made known to you everything I heard from my Father. You did not choose me; I chose you. And I gave you this work: to go and produce fruit, fruit that will last. Then the Father will give you anything you ask for in my name. This is my command: love each other.'

SECTION 3
SPIRITUALITY

The sessions in this section can be used as individual 'one-offs' or as a nine-week series. Looking at various important aspects of spirituality, it begins with an introduction to belief in God and then looks at vital issue-based themes. It concludes with a meeting which looks at a TV programme that has tapped into widespread interest in the paranormal.

1. MEETING GOD
Basic issues relating to belief in God which work well in a group which includes not-yet Christians.

2. WHAT AM I WORTH?
To help young people explore what value God places on each one of them – and how that value doesn't depend on their own abilities, looks or skills.

3. FEAR
Identifies common fears and the negative effect they can have on our lives. Also begins to explore how Christ can set us free from fear.

4. GRACE
This session aims to teach your group what the theological term grace means in theory and practice.

5. HOLINESS
Considers what Christians mean by the word 'holiness' and how holiness is connected to serving God.

6. REBELLION
Examines some of the ways young people rebel (eg against parents), the fact that rebellion has been part of human nature from the very beginning, and the consequences of rebelling against God.

7. ANGELS
Who/what are angels? Their task, how they relate to humans, biblical examples of their mission.

8. THE X-FILES
Growth of interest in the paranormal, ghosts etc. Dangers, biblical warnings, do ghosts exist?

9. SIMPLICITY
The challenge to avoid materialism and live more simply so that others may simply live!

MEETING GOD

MEETING AIM: This session considers some of the basic issues relating to belief in God and will work well in a group which includes not-yet Christians. Be aware that it requires significant preparation in gathering props, including doughnuts and a car number plate!

INTRODUCTION (5 mins)

Say: 'None of us has ever met God face to face yet. However, this is the session when all that will change!'

Sit everybody in a circle and tell those who doubt whether God is there that very soon all their questions will be answered. Have one person take a stopwatch and then get everyone to inhale and hold their breath for as long as they can. Each person should pinch the nose of the person to their right in the circle to prevent cheating! The timekeeper counts aloud as the seconds pass.

Award prizes to the longest breath-holders and reddest faces. Afterwards, ask them why they didn't just continue to hold their breath. Then they would definitely have seen God for themselves!

Talkie Bit: Life was created by God. He designed it to carry on. That's why you open your mouth and breathe! You can't help yourself (hopefully). Death was never part of the plan in God's perfect creation. Deep down, none of us believes in death. Everything inside us tells us that life is not supposed to come to an end. We were created to enjoy eternal life with God.

FAKE IT OR FACE IT (5 mins)

Make copies of the worksheet opposite and hand them out to groups of twos or threes. Make the point that some people misinterpret this inner message about eternal life and try to achieve eternal youth through their own efforts. Get the small groups to list examples of things people do to deny their bodily ageing process (eg dyeing hair, toupée, face lifts), then to list the top 10 celebrity offenders!

DOUGHNUT DISTRACTIONS (3 mins)

Ask: 'So if there is a God-shaped hole inside every one of us, why don't more people do something about it?'

At this point hold up a pack of ring doughnuts. Ask: 'Is anything missing from these doughnuts as doughnuts? No. If you bought one, you'd think you had a perfectly good doughnut.'

Then produce a pack of jam-filled doughnuts. Take a big bite out of one. Then ask the original question again. The answer is yes! The point to make here is that we unthinkingly accept how things are. Life is OK without God for most people, they just accept he's

missing. However, we were never meant to settle for ring doughnuts. God intended us to have a complete jam-centred life! Now give out the remaining doughnuts while reading John 10:10.

PROOF PERFECT (5–10 mins)

Try this little exercise to show that proof is a very hard thing to ultimately produce. First, you need to own a car. Then simply unscrew your car number plate (this sounds worse than it actually is!) and find your MOT certificate. (Be warned you may get into legal problems if you leave your car on a public road without its number plate!)

Produce the car keys in your group and ask: 'Do these prove that I own car registration number ✱✱✱✱ ✱✱✱?' (No, because they could be for any car.)

Then produce the MOT certificate. Ask the same question. (The answer is still 'no' because although the registration number tallies, you could have borrowed the car.)

Finally, hold up the number plates. This will amuse them, but still there's a chance that you might have stolen them...

Make the point that if you don't want to have faith, no amount of evidence will convince you. That is the story of Lazarus and the rich man (Luke 16:20-31). The rich man wanted an angel to visit his brothers so that they would believe, but Abraham basically said: 'They've got enough proof if they really want it.'

THE RIGHT COMBINATION (10 mins)

This sounds dull, but brain-boxes in particular love it. Get a combination bicycle lock. Poke a hole in a clear plastic bag. Put a big bar of chocolate into the bag, and wind the lock through the bag so that the chocolate can only be taken out when the lock is undone.

The point of this visual illustration is that God's endless love for people is something that seems locked up with the key thrown away, but it is available. With a little effort from you, he can help you unlock a love far greater than chocolate. Free love was never God's idea. It is freely available, but it was the most costly of all.

Get the group members one at a time to guess the numbers that make up the four-figure combination. After each guess tell them how many of the four numbers they guessed correctly. When they get all four right, then they have to guess the right order! Whoever finally gets it right can ceremonially unlock the padlock and feast!

YOU'VE GOT A FUNNY WAY OF SHOWING IT! (20 mins)

Get people into small groups of three or four.

Try to ensure that the more outgoing young people are evenly distributed across the groups.

Round One

Provide each team with a newspaper which has a lonely hearts column in it. Give them two minutes to find the most touching and then read it aloud in the most appropriate way. Award marks out of ten. You can also have a 'silliest' round as well.

Round Two

Get everyone on one side of a glass door or low-level window. Get them, in turn, to go to the other side of the window and without shouting mime out 'I love you' to one particular person on your side of the glass. Over-acting is to be encouraged! If the person is convinced, get them to respond appropriately! Marks out of ten.

Round Three

Put up a screen that someone can hide behind. Apart from saying 'Hi', the person behind the screen says nothing throughout. The small groups take turns to stand on the other side of the screen and say, 'I love you,' to the mystery person. Get them to describe themselves, and how exactly they could prove their love to the mystery person. Hopefully the players will get frustrated and try to tempt the hidden person to come out by making ridiculous offers, but the person will refuse them all till the end. The person then reveals who they are – this could prove very amusing! Award points. Tot up final scores from the three rounds and present prizes.

Ask the groups to describe how it felt in each case trying to communicate love, especially when it was hindered by their inability fully to engage with someone who either couldn't or wouldn't respond. Make the point that proving you love someone who is not responding is not only difficult, it is also demoralising.

Then ask the small groups to discuss and come up with answers to these questions:
● How did God prove he loves people?
● Do you think God ever wonders why he bothered when humans don't respond to his holy word (the adverts), put up a barrier between themselves and him (the glass), or worse hide themselves away totally (the screen). What makes him different from us?

Get some feedback from the groups about their answers/comments before moving on.

PICTURING GOD (15 mins)

Say: 'Most people imagine that you can't 'know' someone without seeing them or their photo. But this isn't always true. Imagine that you are suddenly homeless. A family you don't know generously decides to take you in.

You've never met their only son as he has gone travelling. They let you have his room while he is away. He's only taken a few clothes and his own photos with him. Everything else in the room is just the way he left it. Imagine you are very nosey. Look through everything to piece together your own mental picture of the son. Now draw or just list what you've found in the room, and label what the things you've drawn tell you about him.

'How accurate would this profile be? Can you "picture" him? Do you like him?'

Allow up to five minutes for this exercise, then compare profiles with the others in the group.

Say: 'Reading the Bible is a bit like sitting in God's room, reading his personal letters and looking through his sock drawer! Do the Bible bits you know help you "picture" him?

Inevitably you need to ask other people as well whether the son was a good bloke or not. Christians who say they have met with Jesus therefore must tell non-Christians what he's really like.'

Finish this session with a short testimony time, inviting group members to share their experiences of meeting God (you may need to pre-arrange this).

Fake it or face it

Some people try to achieve eternal youth through their own efforts. List examples of things people do to deny their bodily ageing process (eg dyeing hair, toupée, face lifts).

1. _____
2. _____
3. _____
4. _____
5. _____
6. _____
7. _____
8. _____
9. _____
10. _____

List the top 10 celebrity offenders — famous and not-so-famous stars.

1. _____
2. _____
3. _____
4. _____
5. _____
6. _____
7. _____
8. _____
9. _____
10. _____

WHAT AM I WORTH?

MEETING AIM: To help young people explore the value God places on each one of them, and how that value doesn't depend on their own abilities, looks or skills.

GETTING SPICEY (15 mins)

This session uses a Spice Girls theme. You may want to get some members of the group to decorate the venue with posters (readily available from any teen magazine), and have a plentiful supply of their music on tap. Start the session with one or more of these ice-breakers:

● Ask female members of the group to come dressed up as one of the Spice Girls.
● Volunteers in groups of five miming and dancing to a song (you may want to give them time to rehearse).
● (For the daring youth leader only) get five members of the congregation to perform as the Spice Girls.
● (For the kamikaze youth leader only) get the elders of the church to....
● Hold a quiz to find the most knowledgeable on Spice Girls trivia.

SPICE GIRLS OR SUGAR LUMP? (5 mins)

Say: 'Before we look at the truth about how God sees each one of us, it's important to be honest about how we often feel about ourselves. If you look in the mirror, do you really see someone to rival the Spice Girls, or does your heart sink?'

Hand out a pen and a copy of the quiz opposite to each person, to get your youth group thinking along these lines.

I SAID, 'WHO DO YOU THINK YOU ARE?' (15 mins)

Using the answers from the quiz, get the group discussing what they really think of themselves. Many will be happy to talk about what they've put on the quiz sheet, but be sure to respect the rights of others to keep quiet at this point.

Move on to ask what kinds of things make people feel valued or not. Using the different Spice Girls as broad headings, compile five lists on large sheets of paper that you can spread out over the floor.

Ask the group to be as specific as possible, eg rather than just 'mum', what about 'When mum says...' or 'When mum does...'. If anyone introduces something about the way God values us, put it down without comment at this stage.

Sporty Spice: sporting achievements and other abilities and skills
Baby Spice: family and other relationships
Posh Spice: attitudes and inner feelings
Scary Spice: things that don't make you feel valued
Ginger Spice: looks, colour of hair, etc.

I TELL YOU WHAT I WANT, WHAT I REALLY REALLY WANT (15 mins)

We all want to be valued and appreciated. But what happens when all the things on the lists aren't around? What about if you move away to study at college and don't have friends or family close by? What about if you can't play the piano or run like the wind, or don't have a queue of boyfriends/girlfriends waiting at your door? What if you become old? If our sense of value is based on any of those things, we will soon be let down. Ask the group to see if they can imagine circumstances which would mean the things on the list are no longer there to make them feel valued. Cross each one off and see what you have left.

Now for a little action. Arrange for a kidnapping to take place as this part of the meeting goes on. A couple of youth group members, working for the underground organisation Old Spice, can burst in and haul off one of the group, leaving behind a ransom note. (Use your imagination, and sensitivity, to make this as exciting and wacky as possible.) The ransom note should promise the return of the kidnapped member in exchange for a list of items. These should include things like: written promises to do the washing-up at home for a week, small change, etc.

The list of items should be treated seriously and any promises made should be kept (small change can be donated to charity). Of course, your group may decide not to pay the ransom, but that makes a great discussion point in itself!

Break into small groups to consider the following questions and get each group to report back after five minutes:
● How much of a ransom would you be prepared to pay if you really valued/loved the person kidnapped?
● Would you still pay the ransom if you didn't like the person at all?
● How would you feel if you were the one kidnapped and the group paid the ransom for you?
● How would you feel if they decided not to pay the ransom?

Later in the session, you can use this illustration to talk about how much God values us by sending Jesus to die for us.

GIRL POWER OR GOD POWER? (10 mins)

Keep in small groups and encourage them to take a look at some key Bible passages about how God values us, and to think about these three questions:
● Why does God value us?
● How do we know God values us?
● Will God ever stop valuing us?
   1 Peter 1:18–19
   Ephesians 2:6–10
   Luke 15:1–7
   Ephesians 3:14–19

'Girl Power', the catch phrase made popular by the Spice Girls, is about feeling and thinking positively and believing you can do anything. Finish the session by challenging the young people to take on a new catch phrase: 'God Power', knowing that whatever they do, even if they let God down, he'll always value them.

SPICE GIRLS or SUGAR LUMP?

(Circle one statement per question, or add your own comments)

1 Look in the mirror. Do you think:
a) Who on earth is this gorgeous creature waiting to be discovered by the world?
b) Who swapped this mirror for a picture of Frankenstein?
c) I guess it's OK, but if only I could change...
d) (add another comment if you want.) . . . .
. . . .
. . . .

2 You see the person you most want to look like in the school corridor. Do you:
a) Wonder when they put up that mirror?
b) Trip them up?
c) Go home feeling fed up and wonder if you'll ever look like that?
d) (add another comment if you want.) . . . .
. . . .
. . . .

3 Do you spend most of your time feeling:
a) Happy with the way you look?
b) Fed up with the way you look?
c) OK most of the time — until someone says something about you?
d) (add another comment if you want.) . . . .
. . . .
. . . .

4 What would you most like to change about yourself?
a) Your height.
b) Your hair.
c) Your feet.
d) (add another comment if you want.) . . . .
. . . .
. . . .

5 Do you think God loves you for:
a) Who you are?
b) What you do?
c) What you'll become in heaven?
d) (add another comment if you want.) . . . .
. . . .
. . . .

FEAR

MEETING AIM: To help the group identify common fears and the negative effect they can have on our lives, and to begin to explore how Christ can set us free from fear.

It takes much courage to admit to being afraid of things. Be aware throughout this session that the fears individuals voice might mask deeper ones. You'll need to be vulnerable and admit to fears you had as a child, a teenager, and even now.

PREPARATION

Ideally, you need access to 100 young people to play a version of the TV game show *Family Fortunes*. If you're involved in schools work, ask permission to do a survey during a school lunchtime. Otherwise, give your group copies of a simple questionnaire for their friends to fill in. You could always ask people in the church, the answers just won't be as youth-specific. Questions:
1. What are you most afraid of at the moment?
2. Which theme park has the scariest rides?
3. What's the biggest danger facing young people in this area?
Record the top five answers to each question as percentages.

FEAR FACTOR (10 mins)

To introduce the meeting theme in a non-threatening way, hand out copies of the sheet opposite and a pen to each member of your group. Ask them to rate the following situations from one to ten, with one being 'no sweat' and ten being 'totally terrifying'.

Allow about three minutes for the sheet to be completed then get some feedback and discuss their responses and why they chose their ratings. Make the point that people are afraid of different things. What is acceptable for one person may petrify another.

FAMILY FORTUNES (10–15 mins)

Choose two teams of two or three people. Have the questions on OHP, with the top five answers underneath covered so you can reveal them one by one. For each question, one team has to guess what most people replied, getting a point for each correct answer. If they suggest something not in the top five, give the other team a go.

Discuss the answers given in the survey. Were they what the group expected? Do they think people were honest, especially for the first question? Do they agree with the answers?

Draw out the following points:
● Some 'fear' is fun. If they've ever been on a roller-coaster they'll know that queuing up can be terrifying and the ride can be very exhilarating. Point out that however scary a ride may seem, there's no real danger

involved – they're completely safe.
● Some fear is well-founded. Some things are dangerous, and being aware of the danger restrains us and makes sure we're careful, such as looking both ways before crossing a busy road.
● Some fear is irrational. When I was a child I thought there were bees at the bottom of my bed. I practically slept on the pillow so they couldn't sting my feet. You may have a similar 'childhood fear' tale to tell, where the fear has no foundation. Don't belittle those fears, but make the point that some fear has no logic to it.

FEAR-BUSTERS (7–10 mins)

Ask for a volunteer. You also need four scarves or blindfolds. Change these illustrations to ones appropriate to your group. And of course don't talk about these fears as if they are yours if they're not. Use your own!

1. The problem with being afraid comes when fear gets out of control. It rules us and can limit our lives. For example, a friend of mine was terrified of pigeons. She hated being near them in case one flew in her face. So she never went shopping in town. A whole area of life was shut off to her (using a scarf, tie volunteer's feet together).

2. I always used to be afraid that people would laugh at me if I appeared different from them, so I never expressed my own opinions and just went along with the crowd. I missed out on part of being me (tie scarf round volunteer's mouth).

3. Another friend of mine is petrified of flying. A while ago he had to go to Holland for work. But instead of a plane ride that would have taken two hours, it took him a day-and-a-half on the ferry and in a car – much more inconvenient (tie scarf round volunteer's eyes).

4. A fear of water can stop you going swimming, or going boating, or travelling abroad on a ferry. That fear can stop you enjoying whole areas of life (tie scarf round volunteer's hands).

We all experience some kind of fear. But when it gets out of hand it can imprison us and stop us from enjoying life to the full. So what's the answer? How can we rid ourselves of our fears?

We need to understand that Jesus came to set us free from fear. When he first started his ministry, he stood up and announced, 'The Spirit of the Lord is on me because he has anointed me to proclaim good news to the poor, to proclaim freedom for prisoners and sight for the blind' (Luke 4:16–19). Jesus brings freedom to many situations. But one is freedom from fear where fear has imprisoned us. 1 John 4:18 says, 'There is no fear in love.

Perfect love drives out fear, because fear has to do with punishment. The one who fears is not made perfect in love.' Jesus longs to exchange our fears for the security of his love. Then we can enjoy the abundant life he came to give us.

So first, we need to admit we are afraid, realise what that fear is doing to us and how it is restricting our lives (take the blindfold off the eyes).

Second, we should admit the fear to someone else – a friend, a parent, a leader, someone we can trust to get their perspective on it. Often just talking about the fear can make it less powerful (take the scarf off the mouth).

Next, we pray with that friend for Jesus to drive out the fear and replace it with his love. We might need to pray about any events that set off the fear, but we should be confident that Jesus wants to set us free (untie the feet).

Finally, we work to overcome the fear by gradually doing, or getting near, the thing we are afraid of. This takes time, so we must ask our friend to keep praying for us (untie the hands).

Ask your volunteer how it feels to be free – and thank them for their help.

FACING UP TO FEAR (10–15 mins)

We need to be aware of danger, but not live in fear. In groups of two or three, ask your young people to answer these questions about some common fears (use these examples or ones that came up in the survey). Allow at least five minutes for them to work and discuss as small groups, then get them to feed back and compare answers. Ensure that all the groups address the last question before you get feedback and further discussion.
Questions: 1. What is the real danger? 2. How could 'out-of-control' fear make you behave? 3. What is a reasonable response to the danger? 4. What steps could you take to overcome irrational fear?

Common fears: ● fear of being attacked when out ● fear of spiders ● fear of the future – will I get a job? ● fear of being laughed at by your friends ● fear of families breaking up.

HONEST TO GOD (5 mins)

Hand out paper and a pencil to everyone, then ask each person to write down a fear from which they want Jesus to set them free. Reassure them that you'll destroy all the papers at the end of the meeting so no one will see what they write.

Having folded the papers, pass round a bin for the slips. Make this act of binning the fears a prayerful and meaningful moment by praying for each individual out loud, asking that they would know the perfect love of God that drives out all fear.

Fear Factor

Rate the following situations from One (No SWEAT) to Ten (TOTALLY TERRIFYING) - and be honest!

facing your maths teacher when you've failed to hand in your homework on time.

fishing a spider out of the bath.

Owning up to your brother or sister that you've mangled their favourite tape.

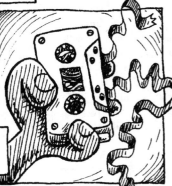

Asking someone out that you fancy.

Standing up in front of your year group at school and taking an assembly.

Walking down a dark unlit street on your own.

Walking barefoot on the patio and treading on a slug.

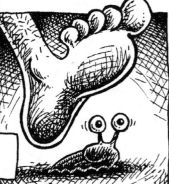

Getting accidentally locked in a very small cupboard.

EAT AT JOE'S

Not being able to get a decent job when you leave school/college/university.

Doing a parachute jump from a plane.

GRACE

MEETING AIM: To teach your group what the theological term 'grace' means in theory and practice.

INTRODUCTION

Communicating theological truth in simple terms requires hard work. Your young people will benefit more if you have a good personal understanding of God's grace.

● Try to include a few 'grace attacks' on the group. For example, as some people go up to the bar/ tuck shop, you personally pay for their drinks/ sweets (no free stock).

● Recommended easy read: *Enjoying God's Grace* by Terry Virgo (Nelson Word/ New Frontiers Publishing).

CODE OF PRACTICE (10 mins)

Announce that you are feeling in an extra generous mood and reward each young person with a packet of sweets. These may only be consumed upon successful completion of the next activity.

The challenge facing the group is to get to the other side of the room by breaking the code, which is initially known only to you. Acting as judge you will award extra sweets for correct moves and make deductions for wrong ones. By taking into account the awards and penalties the young people should be able to crack the code.

Before starting the challenge, quietly inform a small number of young people of the code. It could be something like moving backwards in silence on one leg. Deduct sweets from them if they inform others of the code. Those who fail to fulfil the challenge will be sentenced later.

Ask: 'What would have made the challenge easier to complete?'

GOD IS INNOCENT (5 mins)

We are without excuse. God has clearly communicated the 'code' to us. There is, therefore, no need to guess the way forward. The Bible gives clear indication of how we should live our lives. The problem for us is not what we do not know but what we do know. By ignoring God's guidelines we fail to crack the code of healthy living.

Give, or ask the young people to provide, examples of Christ's values from the Sermon on the Mount [Matthew 5–7].

Ask: 'How easy or difficult is it always to follow this "code"? Knowing that we have all, at some time, failed the code, how might God deal with us?'

GOD IS LOVE (3 mins)

Some say that God is remote and uninterested in our affairs. But 'God is love' (1 John 4:16), and as such he wants the best for us.

Ask: 'How might that response compare to our love for other people?'

WHAT'S YOUR VERDICT? (15 mins)

Distribute copies of the imaginary newspaper report below to each young person and ask them to discuss the follow-on questions.

CHILD ATTACKER IS GUILTY

JEANETTE WAS FOUND UNCONSCIOUS on wasteland less than a mile from her country home. She had been savagely attacked while out playing. Though still alive, she would never be the same again. Jeanette was just eight years old. Neighbours described her as a typical fun-loving kid who adored animals and was popular at school. Her father wept as he told reporters of his daughter's wish to become a veterinary nurse. His grief, however, turned to anger as he admitted that his daughter's injuries meant she would now need special care for the rest of her life.

Initial house-to-house enquiries proved ineffective, yet the police were convinced that the attacker must be a local man. Someone in the village was guilty. Fearing another attack the police decided to take DNA samples from all local males. Being more accurate than a finger print, this would speed up the investigation. Within ten days the police had made an arrest.

Months later John Michael Darby appeared in court charged with attempted murder. The forensic evidence was conclusive. The jury found him guilty and the judge came to pass sentence. To the horror of Jeanette's family John Darby was sentenced to just four years' detention. With good behaviour he could be released after two years. The judge said that he had considered Darby's mental state at the time and his subsequent remorse. Jeanette was in court but unaware of the verdict.

Ask: 'Who, if anyone, in this case experienced justice? Could the judge have responded differently?'

GOD IS JUSTICE (10 mins)

Some say that if God is love then he should let us off when we fail. But God is also justice. To ignore injustice would be to deny his character. This means that the 'guilty' must be punished in order to protect the 'innocent'. God cannot simply let the guilty off, because that would be unjust. The victims, for example, would not accept that justice had been done.

How then can God simultaneously be both love and justice?

Demand that all those who failed the earlier challenge come forward to receive their just reward. This should be delivered in a judicious manner. Each 'guilty' young person should be sentenced to the 'gunge bucket'. This should be filled with suitably disgusting contents, such as custard and baked beans. Make much drama of covering the floor with a protective sheet and, under protest, offer to cover their clothes with plastic bags. These should be woefully inadequate.

In the midst of the hype you, or a co-worker, should openly reaffirm the necessity of the sentence, while assuring the group of your love. Finally, prepare to carry out the sentence, but at the last moment you, the 'innocent' leader, should take the place of the 'guilty' young people. For added effect, your sentence should be carried out by the young people who have just been released.

Make the point that God's justice means the 'guilty' must be sentenced. His love, however, led the innocent Son of God to step in and accept the punishment we deserved. This undeserved favour is God's grace towards us. Nothing we can do can change what God has already done.

Video options:
● *Jesus of Nazareth* (or equivalent); crucifixion scenes or
● Michael W. Smith's *Secret Ambition* available on "2x4" (Word).

GRACE ATTACKS (10 mins)

Many people who have been rescued from danger talk of a subsequent change in lifestyle. Few would risk offence by blatantly returning to the same danger and expecting to be rescued again. Knowing the price of God's grace should result in a change of lifestyle [Romans 6].

Challenge each young person to commit a 'grace attack', bestowing undeserved favour on individuals in the community. Encourage the group to give considerate and imaginative thought to what they might individually do. Examples could include offering to wash people's cars for nothing or paying a local newsagent to allow the next customer(s) to have their newspaper for free.

Make photocopies of the explanatory flyer (opposite) or, alternatively, ask the group to design their own.

When the group next meets, ask the young people to record their grace attacks' anonymously or on a flip-chart (or equivalent). Stress the importance on anonymity and humility and congratulate the group collectively on their efforts.

You've been

GRACE ATTACKED!

At our youth club we have been considering what 'grace' means. We decided it was 'undeserved favour' and that is what we have sought to demonstrate to you. To find out more please contact your local Christian church.

You've been

GRACE ATTACKED!

At our youth club we have been considering what 'grace' means. We decided it was 'undeserved favour' and that is what we have sought to demonstrate to you. To find out more please contact your local Christian church.

HOLINESS

MEETING AIM: To help young people to understand what Christians mean by the word 'holiness', and to think about how holiness is connected to serving God.

GETTING STARTED

Get your youth group to come dressed in their most special clothes – ie clothes they only put on for a really special occasion (make sure you do the same). Also, ask them to bring something they own that they only use for special purposes (it may be a cup and saucer from mum's dinner service, a piece of jewellery, or perhaps a prized football used only for important matches!). Display those items somewhere during the meeting. We'll come back to them, and the reason for dressing up, later on.

AND NOW FOR SOMETHING COMPLETELY DIFFERENT (15 mins)

Once your group knows you're going to take a look at holiness, this game is a useful way to tease out an understanding of what the word means. It's based on the TV game show *Wipe Out*. Admit it, you know the one I mean – only without some of the technical wizardry and resources available to the BBC.

Fix nine sheets of paper to the wall to look like a game show board. Add whatever extras you like to make it look even better. Each piece of paper bears a word or phrase which could describe holiness. In fact, six are correct and three are wrong. Each team playing needs to select one person to play the game for them while they shout out advice. The person selected has six small circles of paper, each with a blob of Blu-tack on the back. They must select six out of the nine that they think are the correct descriptions of holiness.

If they get it wrong, they're told only how many are right, not which ones. The team that completes the challenge the fastest wins. Below are two selections of words, with the correct six in bold. Add more rounds if you want. Webster's Dictionary or Vine's Expository Dictionary are good resources for looking at word definitions from the Bible.

1. **integrity, sacredness, set apart,** desiccated, **purity,** strong, **saintly, godliness,** fearfulness;

2. **righteousness, devotion, piety,** other worldly, psalms, **consecrated, sanctified,** hallelujah, **innocence.**

Once the game is over, look at the words together and talk about what each of them means. One of the group could make a word map. Starting with 'holiness' in the middle of a large sheet of paper, they fill it with phrases or words that come up as you look at the correct answers to the game.

Try and get down to words that everyone can understand. So 'integrity' might link on to 'honesty' which might in turn lead on to slang like 'safe'. You should finish with a sheet covered in linked words or phrases that have something to do with holiness.

This is a good time to explain why everyone is dressed up for the occasion. Holiness is a complex and rich word with various shades and meanings – depending upon whether it's applied to God or Christians. However, perhaps one of the ways it might be summed up is 'living differently for a reason'. We wear special or different clothes for a reason. You might want to ask the group when and why they wear the clothes they are in. God calls us to be special or different on the inside for a reason too.

SAME PLANET, DIFFERENT WORLD (10 mins)

Either together, or in smaller groups, look up these verses to find the answers to these basic questions about holiness:

● What is it? (Ephesians 4:20–24; Galatians 5:22)
● Why do we need to become it? (2 Corinthians 7:1; 1 Thessalonians 4:7)
● What happens if we are it? (Hebrews 12:14; Romans 6:19–23)
● Who helps us become it? (Romans 1:4; 1 Thessalonians 3:13)

NOW THAT'S CLEVER... (10 mins)

To help your group to try and understand what holiness is all about, try this illustration. It may need some practice beforehand. You'll need a white handkerchief, a bottle of iodine (available from chemists), a carton of photographic fixer (available from any photographic retailer for around £1.80) and a couple of bowls.

Fill one with water and one with photographic fixer: they should both look identical. Soak the hankie in iodine before you begin.

The handkerchief represents us. The moment you dip it in water it will go black and it will make the water black too. It's a useful illustration to talk about the way different things in our lives and our world are wrong.

Now try dipping the blackened handkerchief in the photographic fixer. It will immediately turn white again – a picture of what happens when we become Christians.

Finally, dip the handkerchief back into the first bowl of blackened water. It should immediately turn clear again – a picture of how we can affect the world as Christians. Use this illustration to help your group think about why God wants us to be holy.

WHAT DOES IT MEAN FOR ME? (10 mins)

Holiness needs to be much more than a theological idea. It needs to be something your young people can apply and aspire to in their lives. Draw the session to a conclusion by looking at why we need to be holy. The objects the group have brought with them are all used for a special purpose. Get the group to explain why they've brought them and why they are special.

Hand out copies of the sheet 'How can God use me?'. Ask everyone to tick the boxes of the areas they would like God to work in through them. It's not meant to be a definitive or exhaustive list, but it should get them thinking about how they can serve God.

HOW CAN GOD USE ME? (15 mins)

Hand out a photocopy of the sheet opposite and a pen or pencil to every member of the group. Read out the instructions and then allow three minutes for the sheet to be completed.

Now, either together or in smaller groups, ask everyone to look at the boxes they've ticked. Ask them to think of two characteristics that are especially important for them to do that particular things well and two things that would prevent them from doing it well. For example: a listener would need to be caring and loving, but not a gossip or selfish. Work through as many as time allows so that the group can see the connection between holiness and serving God.

AND FINALLY... (8 mins)

These sessions should have given your young people plenty to think about. They may be aware of areas in their lives that need to change as a result of what they've heard. They may feel challenged by the calling of God to be 'set apart for a purpose'. Finish the evening with a time of quiet meditation. A cross or a candle could be placed in the middle of the room.

Give everyone a piece of paper to write down a prayer which expresses their feelings about what they've heard and what they'd like to see changed in their own life. Play a relevant piece of music (try 'Holy' by HOG, Doug Walker and Shine on the *Jumping in the House of God 2* album from Alliance Music).

You may want to give youngsters the chance to read out their prayers. But finish by asking the group to fold up and place their prayers around the cross or candle as a sign that it's not their will power but God who'll enable those prayers to be answered.

HOW CAN GOD USE ME?

Just for a moment, throw caution to the wind and think about what God might do through you. Tick the boxes of things that you think you could do, or would like to do, to serve God.

- ☐ listener
- ☐ pray-er
- ☐ giver
- ☐ helper
- ☐ evangelist
- ☐ school CU helper
- ☐ group leader
- ☐ children's worker
- ☐ letterwriter (for political or spiritual issues or to those in prison, etc.)
- ☐ Bible sharer
- ☐ speaker
- ☐ encourager
- ☐ counsellor
- ☐ befriending the lonely
- ☐ helping the elderly
- ☐ making people feel special and important
- ☐ concern for the poor
- ☐ concern for the world
- ☐ music
- ☐ singing
- ☐ dancing
- ☐ drama
- ☐ poetry
- ☐ practical jobs
- ☐ helping others to hear what God says
- ☐ enthuser
- ☐ artistic
- ☐ working with the handicapped
- ☐ baby-sitting
- ☐ understanding those with family hurts

REBELLION

MEETING AIM: To help the group consider the ways in which young people rebel (eg against parents), the fact that rebellion has been part of human nature from the very beginning, and the consequences of rebelling against God. This session concludes by looking at the positive aspects of rebelling against things like injustice and hypocrisy.

REBEL WITHIN YOUR WALLS (20 mins)

Take a huge sheet of paper (A1 or A0) and get your group to map out the various 'cliques' and 'types' in their town, school or even just in current British youth culture. Start with a picture in the middle of the area you're mapping: a sketch of the school, a picture of the town, a map of the British Isles, etc.

Around that, put up the various groups or types that represent youth culture. Encompass as much information on it as possible. Types you might want to map include gothics, heavy metal, sporty, mega-trendy, arty, computer buffs, etc. Your young people should know more than you about this! Use these questions as a starter for each group or type:

● What do they look like? (Draw something if possible, or get a cutting from a magazine.)
● What kind of music do they listen to?
● What kind of music would make them feel sick?
● Where do they hang out?
● What's important to them?
● What couldn't they care less about?
● What would their parents say about them?
● What would the minister say about them?
● What (if anything) are they rebelling against?

Once the map is finished, get the group to think through some basic questions about what they've put together. It may help to have the questions as headings written out on another large sheet of paper, and have any comments made by the group added under each question. This helps everyone to remember what has been said, and makes it easier to draw out conclusions at the end:

● Why do people get into those groups?
● What other groups have there been in the past – for example when your parents were teenagers?
● What kinds of things are they rebelling against?
● Why do we rebel?

REBEL WITH FAMILY LAWS (5 mins)

Rebelling against parents is something most teenagers can associate with! Now you've mapped out the area where you live and talked about rebellion generally, move on to get your group thinking about how rebellious they are – when it comes to family life.

Give a photocopy of the self-analysis sheet opposite, plus a pen, to each person. Tell them to circle a number from '0' to '10'. (0 meaning they're not rebellious at all, and 10 meaning it's a major source of confrontation). At the end, ask them to add up their scores and discover what kind of teenager they really are (tell them not to take the results too seriously!).

REBEL WITH CLAWS! (5 mins)

To help your group think some more about the way teenagers rebel, try this true or false quiz on them:

1. French teenagers rebel by hanging a chicken's claw from their clothes.
2. In the 1920s it was considered rebellious for children to walk with their hands in their pockets.
3. In the 1960s some teenagers sewed the British flag onto their anoraks.
4. Australian teenagers rebel by sewing buttons into their hair.
5. Cool teenage lads of the 1970s would add ribbon to the bottoms of their jeans.
6. Crisps were invented by the teenage son of a farmer as a rebellion against eating boiled potatoes.
7. Wearing a scarf was a sign of rebellion for teenagers in the early 1980s.
8. In Indonesia, wearing yellow is a sign of rebellion against your parents but, after marriage, is considered a sign of obedience.
9. In the 1970s the coolest teenagers wore Wrangler jeans and cowboy boots.
10. Teenagers in the 1970s showed they didn't care what people thought by having a hanky hanging from their pocket.

Answers: 1. false; 2. false, or every child would have been a rebel; 3. true, a sign of being a Mod was to wear the union jack on your coat; 4. false, are you kidding!; 5. true, ribbon was used to lengthen jeans; 6. false, you'd have to be pretty gullible to get this one!; 7. true, scarves were worn in school without a coat; 8. false; 9. true, sadly that's what we thought looked good in those days; 10. false, since when has a teenager even known what a hanky is?

REBEL WITH FLAWS (15 mins)

Rebellion has been part of human nature from the very beginning. There's something about us that seems to make humans want to rebel against God. This Bible study gives your youngsters a chance to discover this for themselves.

● Why do people rebel against God and what he tells us is right?

Romans 7:14–20 (the sinful nature at work in us)

Psalm 106:24–25 (not believing in God's promises)

Genesis 3:1–7 (temptation)

● What are the results of us rebelling against God?

Psalm 107:12b (no one to help you)
Deuteronomy 31:27–29 (disaster!)
Hosea 7:13–14 (living a lie)
● How does that make God feel?

Isaiah 63:10 (grieves the Holy Spirit – make sure everyone knows what 'grieve' really means)
Ezekiel 20: 8 (God's anger and punishment)
Isaiah 1:2 (a sad father)

REBEL WITH A CAUSE (15+ mins)

Of course, rebellion can be good too. Jesus rebelled against the religious piety and superficiality of his day. As Christians we're called to rebel against the wrong values. Finish the session by getting your group to think about how they can rebel positively against injustice, hypocrisy, materialism and so on. Try working out together the ultimate Christian rebel: if they really wanted to rebel like Jesus did, then…

● How would they treat people?
● What would they own?
● How would they use money?
● What kind of people would they spend time with?
● What would be important to them?
● How would they feel about third world debt, famine, racism, inequality?

Conclude the session by taking time to create a quiet, reflective moment as you slowly read out Romans 12:1–2 to the group. Let the impact of the words sink in before asking your group to write or say prayers about the kind of 'rebels with a cause' they want to be.

OPTIONAL EXTRAS

If you have time, or want to spread the subject over a few meetings, this is a great chance to inspire your group with 'heroes' of the past and present who've been rebels for God. Try one of the following:

Show the video *William Tyndale: God's Outlaw*. It's a longer film and so will best suit youth groups that can sit through the whole hour or so. There are similar films about John Wycliffe and Martin Luther. All of those films can have a huge impact on young people.

Show the video *More Than Champions* about Christian sports stars, introduced by Kriss Akabusi. Both videos should be available from local Christian bookshops or direct from SP Trust (Tel: 01228 512512) and Christians In Sport (Tel: 01865 311211).

Use the excellent book *On Fire For God* (by John Pollock, ISBN 1 8993.53003, Star) to share some of the stories of past Christians who've rebelled against the world and its expectations. There's a chapter devoted to each one. Get your group to put together some drama to illustrate some of the stories. C.T. Studd's is a good example.

HOW REBELLIOUS AM I?

Circle a number from '0' to '10'. (0 meaning you're not rebellious at all, and 10 meaning it's a major source of confrontation).

what clothes you wear	0 1 2 3 4 5 6 7 8 9 10
what music you listen to	0 1 2 3 4 5 6 7 8 9 10
what hobbies you have	0 1 2 3 4 5 6 7 8 9 10
the kind of language you use	0 1 2 3 4 5 6 7 8 9 10
the food you eat	0 1 2 3 4 5 6 7 8 9 10
the people you hang out with	0 1 2 3 4 5 6 7 8 9 10
staying out late	0 1 2 3 4 5 6 7 8 9 10
what TV you watch	0 1 2 3 4 5 6 7 8 9 10

Add up your score and find out what kind of rebel you are:

0–20 Hey, you're just so nice…your parents have life easy
20–40 Fairly obedient with just a flash of rebelliousness
40–60 Rebel at heart: you don't like being told what to do
60–80 Rebel with a cause – you make life interesting at home

Don't take these results too seriously!

REBEL

ANGELS

MEETING AIM: To enable the group to think biblically and realistically about the topic of angels; to equip them to meet the woolly pop-occult concept which is popular today; to show the bearing of this topic on the way we live our Christian lives. Be careful to keep this session as interactive as possible. By its nature it involves the transmission of a lot of information, and it mustn't simply turn into a lecture.

ANGELIC ALIENS (10 mins)

Give most people a slip of paper with these instructions written on it: 'WARNING! SOME MEMBERS OF THIS GROUP ARE NOT AS THEY SEEM. THEY MAY LOOK LIKE YOUR FRIENDS, BUT ARE ACTUALLY ALIEN IMPOSTORS WHO HAVE EATEN YOUR FRIENDS AND TAKEN OVER THEIR BODIES. YOUR MISSION, SHOULD YOU ACCEPT IT, IS TO MINGLE WITH THE GROUP, CHAT WITH OTHER PEOPLE, AND IDENTIFY THOSE WHOM YOU BELIEVE TO BE ALIENS. YOU WILL RECOGNISE THEM BY TWO SLIGHTLY UNUSUAL HABITS WHICH THEY HAVE.'

Give two or three others an identical slip which reads: 'YOU ARE AN ALIEN. TELL NOBODY. NEVER ADMIT IT. ACT LIKE ALL THE HUMANS DO. BUT WHEN YOU CHAT WITH HUMAN BEINGS YOU MUST:

(a) SCRATCH YOUR NOSE EVERY TIME YOU SAY 'NO';

(b) MAKE A COMMENT ABOUT FOOD EVERY TIME THERE IS A LULL IN THE CONVERSATION.

Then let the group mingle and chat for a few minutes. Warn them that the aliens will not reveal their identity, and the humans should not voice their suspicions. They should simply carry on talking.

After some time, call the group together and ask for votes on who the aliens are. Ask what the two unusual habits were. Then ask the aliens to reveal themselves.

Say: 'Is it possible that there are hidden outsiders among us here on earth? Not man-eating aliens, but maybe something more friendly?'

Read this excerpt from Karen Goldman's best-selling *The Angel Book*:

We must not think angels have been hiding from us simply because we haven't known where or how to look for them. Angels have always been our friends and gentle assistants. They are not only in books, on Christmas trees and cathedral walls; they are among us every day of our lives. They are not only on the periphery of our lives; they are with us now, if we would only recognize them. If you seek an angel with an open heart, you shall always find one. On earth, an angel's wings are inside.

Explain how this has become a popular idea over the last few years, but that:

● New Agers speak of their 'guardian angels' who assist their spiritual journey.

● There's an Internet site (http://www.netangel.com) where people send in stories of angel encounters, and buy angel sweatshirts and souvenir mugs!

● Several popular films have exploited the idea of angels appearing to humans and helping them (see if the group can name any!)

● There are magazines such as Angel Times, Angels on Earth and Celestial Voice, dedicated to spreading the news that angels are real.

Tonight we ask: 'What does the Bible say about this subject?'

WINGING IT (10 mins)

Find out what people already know by playing *Call my Bluff* (in which three people offer competing definitions of the same word or phrase – one of which is correct, two of which are rubbish – and the audience guess who is right). Here are the 'true' definitions. Make up some plausible false ones for yourself!

ANGEL – Greek word meaning 'messenger'. An angel brings communications from God.

ARCHANGEL – Seemingly, a superior angel, but we don't have any real information in Scripture.

CHERUBIM – A name given to one kind of angel seen by Isaiah.

GUARDIAN ANGEL – Angel who has a particular responsibility for one human being. Phrase not used in the Bible.

FALLEN ANGELS – Rebels against God, now bound in chains and awaiting condemnation (Jude 6).

Sum up what you've covered:

Angels are messengers from God, doing his will (Psalm 103:20). In heaven they see God's face (Matthew 18:10) and praise him (Revelation 4:5; Isaiah 6). They appear to be ordered in ranks (1 Thessalonians 4:16), and to be of different types, but we don't know much about this. There seems to have been a rebellion at one point; perhaps this is linked with the fall of Satan, which Isaiah 14 and Ezekiel 28 seem to discuss. And there seem to be evil angels (Daniel 10:20–21) who conflict with God's forces. But no information is clearly given. There may be individual angels who look after individual humans (Matthew 18:10; Acts 12:15), but we aren't directly told.

Say: 'God has left us in a lot of uncertainty, hasn't he! This is because we don't need to understand angels too clearly – just receive their help. But some things are clear.'

ANGELS AND INSECTS (15 mins)

Draw two intersecting circles on a large piece of paper. One represents the natural world, the other the spiritual world.

Say: 'There are some created beings who live only in the natural world, without any spiritual life. We call them "animals". Human beings live in the intersection: we have both a physical life and a spiritual life. Angels live in the other circle. They're purely spiritual beings. They can appear in a human form; but they aren't human, or animal. They're different.'

Divide into small groups, and give each group a number of cards, each containing the name of one incident in Bible history. Say: 'Angels were involved in some of these incidents, and not in others. Try to swap cards with the other groups so that you end up with a set containing as many angel incidents as possible.'

After a few minutes, call them together and check the results. (Good 'angel incidents' to use might be: creation; birth of Jesus; Jesus' baptism; Peter's release from prison; Lot's escape from Sodom; the ascension; Balaam's ass; the end of the world.)

Make the point that angels have been God's instruments throughout history. If we're Christians, they have a special ministry to help us (Hebrews 1:14). But we mustn't become obsessed with them. They flit in and out of the picture quietly without drawing attention to themselves. So the question is: How do we relate to angels?

ARE YOU BEING SERVED? (15 mins)

Now give each small group a pen and a photocopy of the sheet opposite. They will also need at least one Bible per group. Give them five to 10 minutes, then get some brief feedback.

Sum up by saying: 'Angels are often invisible, and often look completely ordinary; they're just created beings like us, and must not be worshipped. In fact, we have privileges they don't. We are part of God's family, and the angels are detailed to look after us. Our authority in God's kingdom will be much greater than theirs – because we belong to Jesus.'

LOW-FLYING ANGELS (10 mins)

Discuss: 'If these things are the truth about angels, how should it make us feel?'

Conclude by saying: 'We can be truly thankful for the ministry of angels; yet we must realise we live in a world at war with God. Sometimes we have to be willing to take up the cross and suffer for our faith. And angels won't take the challenge out of Christian living for us.'

angels

Read this statement and see how many errors you can identify. Circle the errors.

'You can always tell angels because of their wings and white clothes. When you see one, you should fall down immediately and worship it, otherwise you'll get fried. Jesus was one of the angels himself, indeed the biggest one. Angels can be really useful because you can get them to do whatever you want, just like a genie in a bottle. But we should be careful with angels. One day they will help God judge us at the end of the world!

Once you have completed this exercise look up these scriptures to see if you were right, or if you missed some:

● Hebrews 13:2
● Colossians 2:18
● Revelation 19:9-10
● Hebrews 1:4-5
● Psalm 103:20
● 1 Corinthians 6:3

THE X-FILES

MEETING AIM: This session aims to give a general biblical approach to the paranormal. It doesn't try to explain all the phenomena. Be careful not to allow it to become a ghost-story-swapping session! Read up on the subject beforehand – you can make your presentation much stronger by having a few factual illustrations. Watch out for people who are especially affected by it (eg, unusually frightened, or unexpectedly well informed) and be prepared to have some personal chats later if necessary. Aim to leave people with an impression of the power and authority of the gospel – not the fascination and allure of the occult.

WHAT'S IN THE X-FILES? (10 mins)

Begin by telling the group a couple of strange stories (eg, an encounter with a UFO). In small groups, have a competition to see who can write the longest list of paranormal phenomena (eg, ghosts, astrology, astral travel, fortune telling, curses and jinxes, levitation).

Combine lists on a flip chart. Point out that this is a massive area and you won't cover all (or most) of these things in this session. For many there are no definite explanations anyway, but we know enough about X-Files material to be able to lay down some general rules.

Look at the list again, and grade each item from 0 (= 'I don't believe in this at all') to 5 (= 'This really happens and the evidence proves it').

Inevitably, people will disagree widely. Discuss the results, without getting drawn into detailed discussion. Point out that this subject fascinates because we have to do a lot of guesswork. Opinions clash because there are few answers. (Use a video clip to demonstrate how The X-Files constantly sits on the fence and refuses to give definite conclusions!)

Say: 'There are three broad explanations for paranormal phenomena, and we need to bear them in mind when looking at any one claim…'

Mulder and Scully from BBC tv's *The X-Files*

THE TRUTH IS OUT THERE…POSSIBLY (10 mins)

Perform a simple but baffling magic trick. For example, find three volunteers, and claim you can read their minds. Ask them to concentrate silently on a Christmas present they received last year; you will pick up their thoughts and write down what they are thinking about.

No. 1 concentrates hard, and after a moment you write something down, and seal it in an envelope. You ask him to tell the group what he was thinking about, so that they can check later whether you got it right. You do the same with No. 2 and No. 3. You hand out the envelopes. You have written down their thoughts exactly.

The secret? No. 3 is a 'plant'. You have already agreed secretly what he will say. So the first thing you write down is his statement, pretending to write down No. 1's. Then No. 1 tells the group what he was thinking about, and you simply write it down next time! Do the same with No. 2, and you have three envelopes all containing correct predictions!

Tell them the secret, and make the point that we can be fooled more easily than we think. Conjurers rely on the fact that their audience secretly wants to believe. So many 'paranormal' effects are actually fakes, or the product of wishful thinking.

THINKING GOD'S THOUGHTS (10 mins)

Now get someone to read out this story, which contains three things that just don't happen in science. Ask the group to spot what they are.

It was evening, and the professor's assistant was clearing up the lab. As he did so, he sighed wearily. It had been another frustrating day. All week he had been trying to combine two chemicals, and they just wouldn't co-operate. On Monday and Tuesday they had turned green and melted together. On Wednesday when he applied exactly the same amount of heat, they had turned blue, exploded and burned his eyebrows off. On Thursday nothing had happened, and on Friday – today – they had simply vanished from the test tube and reappeared in the fridge. He hated it when chemicals did that. Of course, for the professor it worked every time; he was a specially gifted sensitive and scientific materials naturally obeyed him. It just wasn't fair. He packed his briefcase and switched off the lights. Maybe he ought to give it up and work for Sainsbury's.

Discuss the story. The three things are: (a) scientific experiments are reliably repeatable, and work in exactly the same way on every day of the week; (b) you don't have to be specially gifted to achieve results, because God's creation works in a regular way; (c) materials don't vanish and reappear – they follow rules of cause and effect.

Science would be impossible if we couldn't confidently predict results, and expect the same thing to happen in all circumstances.

Make the point that paranormal events often don't work like this – which makes us suspect they aren't 'proper' science. But when they do, it may just be that we are observing a genuine scientific principle we simply don't understand yet. Read together Genesis 1:28 and Psalms 8:4–8. At creation, God didn't issue the human race with a manual covering every aspect of science; he left us to explore and understand his creation. One great scientist this century said that science was simply 'thinking God's thoughts after him'.

Give examples – some practices in alternative medicine seem to work reliably, although we don't know why. Maybe someday we will. Many simple hauntings seem to follow regular rules; you don't have to be specially sensitive to experience them. Perhaps they are a kind of optical illusion we don't really understand, and really nothing at all to do with dead people floating around. Déjà vu (when you feel you've been somewhere before, or you have a sudden premonition of what someone is just about to say) seems to be explained by a 'disrhythmic functioning' of the two lobes of your brain (see the Encyclopedia Britannica article on the subject).

SCREWTAPE'S PARTY TRICKS (10 mins)

But many phenomena are neither fake nor repeatable science. We have to be careful, because the Bible says there is a realm of reality which is dangerous and hostile to human life (read together Ephesians 6:12 and 1 John 4:1), and it's possible to contact this area.

In small groups, discuss briefly:

1. Why is the paranormal so fascinating to people who don't believe in any religion or supernatural reality?

2. If you were the devil, how would you use the paranormal to ensnare people?

Compare results. Make two points: first, people are fascinated with this area because we all have a craving for spiritual reality, to find something bigger than us, and that leaves people vulnerable to all sorts of deceptive forces. Second, the devil is too bright to use the same route every time. So not everybody who plays with a ouija board, or consults an astrologer, will be deeply affected by it – and people will say, 'Oh, I did that, but it was just a game. It doesn't harm you.' But the danger always exists, and often a user will be really damaged.

X-FILES AND THE BIBLE (15 mins)

End this session with a Bible study. Break into

small groups, hand out a pen and a photocopy of the sheet opposite. They will also need at least one Bible per group. Give them up to 10 minutes, then get some feedback. and look at these questions, then combine results:

FINALLY (5 mins)
It's important to end a sensitive session like this in prayer, re-emphasising the authority and protection of Jesus Christ in this whole area of reality. Thank God for the spiritual safety and certainty we possess, and pray for those who are being deluded by dangerous alternatives. Offer to meet and talk with anyone who still has some personal questions to sort out, or experiences they need to discuss.

X-FILES AND THE BIBLE

Look up these Bible passages and then try to answer the questions:

1 | Isaiah 8:19–22

- What is God's attitude to people trying to gain information through paranormal insight and contacting the dead?

- How can you tell whether an utterance is true?

- What's the end result of taking this route? What's a better source of reliable guidance?

2 | Acts 19:13–20

- What can happen when you try to use supernatural powers without the right authority?

- What authority do demons recognise?

- What's the best thing to do if you have been involved with occult practices in the past?

3 | Revelation 20:8

- What's the end result of people who try to control the supernatural world?

- Why are they lumped together with the other types of people on this list – what's the common factor?

SIMPLICITY

MEETING AIM: To help young people think about their lifestyle in the light of Matthew 6:25–33. To challenge the materialistic assumptions of Western youth culture and create a vision for a simple, attractive, worry-free way of living.

Be careful not to use this session to make everyone feel helplessly guilty! If they end up feeling condemned, they're unlikely to respond positively!

PREPARATION

Before the meeting, prepare in any one of these three ways:

a) Ask the group to keep a record, for one week, of all the money they spend. Ask them to note it down under 'essential' (eg bus fares to school, buying lunch), 'reasonable' (eg an ice cream on a hot day) and 'extravagant' (eg a new 45 top). Tell them that the information will be for their eyes only.

b) Challenge three of them to spend 10 hours (in daylight) on the streets, with only 50p to keep them going. (You'll need parental permission for this!) They are not allowed to go home, or to a friend's house. They must not beg. But they must keep a diary of what happened, and how they felt.

c) Video a room in your house. Zoom in on consumer items you have lying about. (Plant some there if necessary.) The idea is to get a snapshot of your possessions.

Also; rewrite Matthew 6:25–33 in your own words. Make it as unlike 'Bible-speak' as you can, so that they won't recognise it.

Resources: Many of the facts in this outline came from just one issue of New Internationalist magazine – a vital resource on matters of world need, consumerism and lifestyle. The magazine has a web site at http://www.newint.org/. Other useful web sites: http://www.oneworld.org (the best), http://envirolink.org/issues/enough/index.html, http://www.greenpeace.org, http:// www.wasteweb.com/swap, and http://www.speakeasy.org/new.

Books: try Michael Redclift, *Wasted* (Earthscan); Alan Durning, *How Much is Enough?* (Earthscan); Ronald Sider, *Rich Christians in an Age of Hunger* (Hodder).

INTRODUCTION (5 mins)

Read your version of Matthew 6 to the group and ask for comments. After a while, reveal that these aren't just anybody's ideas – they come from Jesus!

Say: 'Tonight we are going to explore whether Jesus' thinking makes sense. First, let's take a look at the world we live in...'

A REALLY RUBBISH QUESTIONNAIRE (5 mins)

Hand out photocopies of the questionnaire opposite, along with pens. Allow three minutes for them to be completed, and then announce the answers. The answer in every case is (c).

Say: 'The incredible waste in our world is accelerating, not slowing down. If everyone on the planet lived as we do, the earth would be a burned-out shell within thirty years. Christians who believe this world is God's creation ought to be in the forefront of developing a different lifestyle.'

SMARTIE POWER! (5–10 mins)

Give everybody a few Smarties. Ask them to go up to other people at random and ask to see their Smarties. The person with more Smarties is given a Smartie by the other person, except that:

a) somebody with an orange Smartie always wins over someone without an orange Smartie;

b) someone with a blue Smartie always wins over someone with an orange Smartie;

c) someone with both orange and blue must give away one of those to the first person who asks.

When the game starts running out of steam, call a halt, and discuss. Who is winning? Why? The answer: it depends on the hand you start with. If you begin rich, you become richer (unless you're stupid). Say: 'It's the same in our world – the rich keep getting richer. Jesus wants us to live simply because of the needs of the world.'

INSECURITY (10 mins)

Also, the more we have, the more we worry. Divide into small groups. Tell them someone has died and left them a massive mansion with a swimming pool. What new worries do they now have? Make a list (eg upkeep of the building, heating bills, insurance, staff, maintenance of the pool, security...).

Compare lists, and make the point that Jesus wants us to live simply because wealth brings worries.

POOR LITTLE RICH BOY (10 mins)

But there's a deeper reason yet. In groups, look at these verses, and answer the question: Why does the Bible see lots of possessions as a bad thing? James 5:1–3; 1 Timothy 6:8–10; Philippians 4:12–13).

Compare results.

Sum up: Jesus wants us to live simply because too many good things are a trap for us. They distract us from the most important thing in life: living for God's kingdom.

SO HOW DO YOU DO IT? (10 mins)

Stress that we're not talking about vows of total poverty. Jesus had wealthy followers. Early Christians like Onesiphorus and Philemon used their wealth to help other Christians. We're talking about adopting a reasonable lifestyle that uses God's creation responsibly.

If you used preparation idea (a), ask them to look at their lists. Do they reflect the kind of simple lifestyle Jesus was talking about?

If you used idea (b), get your 'homeless' people to share some of their diaries. How did it feel suddenly to be stripped of lots of things you take for granted?

If you used idea (c), show the video twice, and on the second run-through, ask them to pause the film whenever they notice something you might be able to do without!

The group should end up discussing what is and isn't essential for a sensible but simple lifestyle in our culture.

Inject some questions:

● Do we need to buy designer labels, or should Christians go for cheaper alternatives?

● How much confectionery and Coke is compatible with a simple lifestyle?

● How much should we spend on Christmas presents for other people?

Try to work out together five practical things people could do to inject more simplicity into their lifestyle. Write them on a large poster. Get group members to sign their name by anything they will try out for a month. Four weeks later, you will discuss how it went, whether to continue, and what other ideas have come to mind.

Close in prayer, asking God to help you with this exercise and to teach you more about simplicity. Ask him to make himself more real to you as you learn to trust a little more in him.

A REALLY RUBBISH QUESTIONNAIRE

1. How many tons of printed paper are produced each year by the United Nations?
(a) 15 tons
(b) 138 tons
(c) 270 million tons

2. What is the most expensive component of a can of Coke?
(a) The water which makes up 90% of it
(b) The secret ingredient known only to Coca Cola
(c) The can

3. By the year 2005, how many old computers will be buried in landfill sites in America?
(a) Enough to fill the White House
(b) Enough to fill a baseball stadium including the seats
(c) Enough to fill a football field a mile high

4. How many TV sets are there in the world?
(a) 100 million
(b) 500 million
(c) 800 million

5. How much paper and plastic tableware is used in North America every year?
(a) Enough to provide a picnic for everyone in the Third World
(b) Enough to stretch from Paris to Warsaw
(c) Enough to feed the whole world a picnic every other month

SECTION 4
EVANGELISM & MISSION

These meetings could radically change you and the young people you work with! That's not because they contain creative strategies - although they do! It's because God could radically transform the outlook and faith levels of you and your young people as you explore what the Bible says about the people who live around you in your community and in the wider world.

A key part of these meetings aims to alter our perspective so we see other people the way God sees them. It also holds a challenge to reach out to our peers, to serve the elderly, the hurting and build cross-cultural bridges. It should also help trigger prayer on a world-wide perspective. Through all seven meetings there is a strong emphasis on 'doing' with practical projects for the young people to get stuck into.

Your young people and you too may never be the same again!

1. SEEING THROUGH GOD'S EYES
Evangelism and service depend on our seeing other people the way God sees them

2. PEER EVANGELISM
Challenging young people to reach out to their peers

3. GOLDEN OLDIES
Caring for and serving the elderly of the community

4. ACROSS THE CULTURES
Building cross-cultural bridges

5. HELPING THE HURTING
To teach that a key motive for evangelism is love

6. WORLD-CLASS PRAYER
Praying for the whole world, not locked into our own little world

7. WORLD-CLASS COMPASSION
Balancing compassion with practical involvement

SEEING THROUGH GOD'S EYES

MEETING AIM: Mission depends on our seeing other people the way God sees them. This session will help young people realise that every person is loved by and precious to God. We all tend to ignore or even criticise people who are not part of our peer group, but such alienation is especially true among teenagers. While belonging is vitally important to each of them, they are still very slow to reach out to new people. This session will show that such hesitancy is normal, but must be overcome by seeing people the way God sees them.

GRAFFITI BOARD (10 mins)

Using a chalkboard, OHP or a long piece of paper taped to the wall, get your young people to respond to the question: 'What current examples can you give of people feeling good about themselves by defeating or putting someone else down?' You may want to prime the pump with examples from politics, sports, or advertising. You may want to refer back to this later in the meeting, so leave their answers up.

PRUI (10 mins)

This game illustrates the infectious magnetism of reaching out, but you should not cite this point until after the game is played. The Prui (pronounced PROO-ee) is a gentle, friendly creature that grows. If you want to get people in touch (literally) and feeling comfortable with each other, introduce them to the Prui.

Everyone stands in a group, closes their eyes and starts milling about. When you bump into someone, shake his/her hand and ask, 'Prui?' If the other person asks 'Prui?' back, then you have not found the Prui. Keeping your eyes closed, find another person to ask.

When everybody is bumping about, shaking hands, with strains of 'Prui? Prui? Prui?' floating around the crowd, you whisper to one of the players that he or she is the Prui. Since the Prui can see, this person should open their eyes. It seems that the Prui is also a smiling mute, for when someone bumps into him, shakes his hand, and asks that gentle question, he doesn't respond. Ask again, just to make sure: 'Prui?' No response. Eureka, you've found the Prui at last!

Now you can open your eyes. You're part of the Prui too. Keep holding the Prui's hand, and when someone bumps into you, shake with your free hand and don't respond when he or she asks. That's how the Prui grows.

Explain that they can only shake the Prui's hand at either end, so if you bump into two clasped hands, you know you've got the Prui somewhere in the middle. Feel your way to the end and join it.

Soon enough, everybody's happily holding hands except one or two lost souls groping their way along the line of bodies. When the last stray joins up and opens their eyes, the smiling Prui usually breaks the silence by letting out a spontaneous cheer.

('Prui' is from *The New Games Book* by Andrew Fluegelman. © 1976 by Headlands Press, Inc. Reprinted by permission of Doubleday & Company, Inc.)

IDENTIFICATION GAME (5–10 mins)

Say: 'In our culture, we often discover that we do not feel so good about ourselves (the way we look, our performance, etc). To overcompensate for our low feelings, we put other people down by criticising or making fun of them. Sociologists call this action by technical names ending in 'ism' that refer to the people or group being downgraded. Can you work out these technical names?'

Discriminating against a young or old person (ageism)

Putting people down because of their ethnic background (ethnism)

Thinking or acting unkindly towards the other gender (sexism)

Defaming people because of their economic status (classism)

Ridiculing or hurting people because of their race (racism)

You can add to this game by having people make up their own 'isms', like 'nerdism' or 'grades-ism'.

After sharing the answers, discuss recent examples they have seen (or done themselves) that are manifestations of these 'isms'. At this point, just listen to examples without passing judgement. Let the Bible study do the judging.

STROLL THROUGH SAMARIA (20 mins)

Say: 'Jesus confronted all of these types of judgemental attitudes when he walked the earth. One of the most prominent examples occurs in John 4.' Read these passages one at a time and ask the following questions:

1) John 4:1–4
● Jesus had to pass through Samaria. Does anyone know what would be difficult about Jesus. a Jew, going through the region of Samaria?' (Samaritans were half-Jew and half-Gentile, and the Jews hated them.) You might also point out here that Jesus' trip through Samaria was unusual. Most Jews would have taken an extra two-day trip out of their way to the east to avoid Samaria and the Samaritan people.

2) John 4:5–9
● Why is it unusual that Jesus spoke to the Samaritan woman? (First, she was a Samaritan, and Jews and Samaritans did not talk. Second, she was a woman, and men and women of that time did not just strike up conversations.)
● What is unusual about the time of day for the woman to be drawing water at a well? (It was a desert-like area, and to be coming to a well at noon was most unusual. Most people would come to a well to draw water early in the day before it was hot. The woman here was obviously coming at an unusual time to avoid seeing other people, especially since the regular time for going to the well was also a social time for the village women.)

3) John 4:10–15
● Jesus talked about living water and the woman talked about regular water. Why do you think that the woman didn't seem to get the message? (Jesus seemed to talk in codes that she didn't understand.)

4) John 4:16–19
● To continue to explain things to this woman, Jesus changed the subject to her marital status. Why do you think he did this? (He wanted her to confront her sin, and he wanted to let her know that he knew why she was coming to the well at an odd hour – her marriage record and her current live-in lover would have made her the subject of others' gossip.)

5) John 4:20–26
● Why do you think the woman started to change the subject? (She probably felt that Jesus was getting too personal with His questions about her husbands.)
● Jesus told the woman about worship being related to the worshipper rather than the place. How might this apply to us? (It reminds us that worship is not restricted to church services or buildings.)
● The woman stated her understanding of a coming Messiah. Jesus revealed himself as that Messiah. What does it say about Jesus that he would present Himself as the Messiah to this woman? (It shows that he is the Saviour [Messiah] of all people, and he looks at people based on their need for 'living water' [eternal life] rather than on their gender, racial or ethnic backgrounds, or even their sinful pasts.)

SUM UP (10 mins)

Say: 'As we watch Jesus relate to the Samaritan woman at the well, we learn three things about the way in which God relates to us and sees us.'

1) God sees us as valuable and in need of his love, despite our past. Jesus identified the sin of the woman (her adulterous lifestyle), but he never rejected her based on her past sins. He presented himself as the Saviour/Messiah, regardless of her past.

Use the worksheet opposite to illustrate the point that God will forgive our sins. Pass out pens and copies of the sheet to everyone and have group members write down (privately) what they think is their worst sin or sins. Then tell them that if Jesus is their Saviour, God sees Jesus – not their sins. Have them write the name 'Jesus' over their sin list. Because of Jesus, they can crumple the paper up and throw it away! Pass around a metal bin to collect the crumpled sheets, then drop a lighted match into the bin and burn up the sheets. Be careful not to start a fire and don't perform this near or under a smoke alarm! Using a personal testimony might be effective at this point.

2) God does not love us based on the standards of a sinful society. We might feel like losers (like the woman, who came to the well alone because she had no friends), or we might feel judged because of something like our race or gender or ethnic background. God sees us as we are and loves us irrespective of our background. Try to add illustrations (getting dropped from a sports team, failing an exam, etc) that your group can identify with.

3) When we realise that God's love for us is not based on our backgrounds and that he forgives our sins, we can start to see ourselves and other people from God's perspective. He sees us all as in need of the Saviour Jesus, and he sees us all as precious and valuable.

Have your group think of or list a 'Samaritan woman-type' person in their lives whom they need to start reaching out to. Encourage them to think about a person they have not regarded as valuable, and challenge them to start seeing that person as God does.

Closing with a time of conversational prayer is helpful, especially if the group are willing to confess before God that they have not been seeing themselves as he sees them. Thanking God for sending Jesus for us, in spite of ourselves, and asking God for power to reach out to people we have not been loving reminds the group that outreach is based on seeing ourselves and others from God's perspective.

OPTIONAL EXTRAS

1) It might be useful to supplement this session with a study of Psalm 139 to give your group a better perspective on their special place in God's eyes.

2) Follow up next week by asking the group if they made contact with the person they listed or thought of under Point 3 of 'Sum up'.

Write down on this sheet what you think are the worst things (sins) you have committed. DON'T WORRY this sheet will not be read by anyone else and will be destroyed shortly.

My worst sins are...

_____

_____

_____

_____

_____

_____

_____

_____

_____

_____

_____

_____

_____

_____

_____

_____

PEER EVANGELISM

MEETING AIM: To show that the best person to reach your friends is you. This session challenges young people to start reaching out to their closest peers.

DUE SOUTH (10 mins)

Using an agree/disagree format, ask the group to respond to this statement: 'Considering that God wants to reach the whole world with the love of Christ, and in light of the fact that most of the people who have never heard of Jesus are in India, China and Muslim countries, every British Christian should plan to be a missionary.'

After your young people decide whether they agree or disagree, get them into two groups to debate with each other in an effort to win people to their side. If one position is not taken, then you take it. Groups can use statistics, the Bible and opinions in an effort to defend their views.

FRIENDSHIP EVANGELISM QUESTIONNAIRE (10–15 mins)

Pass out copies of the survey form opposite to your young people and ask them to complete it and tally their scores.

You may or may not want to collect these forms in. The feedback from the group should tell you who, if any, in your youth group has non-Christian friends they are trying to witness to. Close this opener by discussing for two to three minutes.

Say, 'What do you think it says about us if all of our closest friends are already Christians? How can we start making friends with non-Christians?'

TWENTY-FIRST-CENTURY UPDATE (15–20 mins)

Have your youth group break into small groups, then assign them the task of reading and 'updating' the following passages:

Group 1 – Mark 5:1–20

Compose a sketch in which a professional actor's agent discusses the story with the healed demoniac. The agent should retell what happened to him, and suggest speaking, writing, acting and other options that are now open to the man. The sketch should close with the healed demoniac making a decision based on verse 19.

Group 2 – Matthew 9:9–13

Write an article about Jesus and Matthew for the News of the World newspaper. Include the response of Jesus, and the author's opinions of why Jesus did what he did.

Group 3 – Matthew 4:18–20

Bring this up to date with a sketch that shows some modern equivalents of what it means to be 'fishers of men and women'. Remember to find contemporary jobs for the ones who are called and show what happens when they leave their jobs 'immediately'.

Group 4 – John 1:35–42

Conduct a 'man-on-the-street' interview with Andrew. Ask him questions about Jesus, the words of John, and why he went first after his brother, Simon Peter.

THINK LOCAL (5 mins)

Say: 'We sometimes think that the task of reaching out belongs to the missionary or the pastor. We can even find ourselves being more concerned about the world's starving people than we are about the people we call our best friends. We can find ourselves caring only about people we don't know.'

The example of Jesus and the people who followed him was that they went first to the people right around them:

1. The healed demoniac was told to go to his own people and tell them what the Lord had done.

2. Andrew went immediately to his brother, Simon Peter.

3. Jesus encouraged Matthew to bring his friends together so that he could be with them, even though they were despised in society.

4. Peter and Andrew and James and John were called by Jesus to be 'fishers of men and women', to extend their 'nets' to the people around them and bring them in to Jesus.

We too must start where we are reaching out to the people around us.

TAKING ACTION (15 mins)

Say: 'Now that we have looked at Jesus and the others who started reaching out by going first to the people they knew, we need to think about ourselves.' (Added illustrations out of your own life greatly enhance the points you have just made and prepare the group to apply the truths themselves.)

Have the group fill out the Friendship Evangelism Action Response (opposite). After these responses are completed have someone (who you asked before the meeting) give a testimony of how God has used him or her in a friendship evangelism role.

OPERATION ANDREW (10 mins)

This final activity can be used to prepare for what is called an 'Andrew Dinner'.

Using the example of Andrew in John 1, you can encourage young people to start praying about and pursuing a 'Simon' who they can invite to a dinner sponsored by the youth group. Like Andrew, your young people's role will be to bring people to a place where they can be introduced to Jesus (through the programme and speaker surrounding the dinner). (Alpha Meals/Suppers are a similar concept.)

It doesn't have to be a formal dinner, you may prefer an all-night lock-in or some other social organised by the group.

Spend some time brainstorming ideas for the meal/supper. Remember – unless the young people like the idea and buy into it, they won't invite their friends.

Evangelism Questionnaire

1. List three people you consider your closest friends (outside of your youth group or your family):

i. _____

ii. _____

iii. _____

Score 10 points per friend   TOTAL _____ (a)

2. Of these three, how many...

know that you are a Christian? _____

have you ever invited to church? _____

know that you read the Bible? _____

have you invited to youth group? _____

have you directly witnessed to? _____

TOTAL _____ x 10 points each = TOTAL _____ (b)

3. Of these friends, how many are already Christians? _____

= TOTAL _____ (c)

Your Friendship Evangelism Quotient (a) + (b) − (c) = _____

Friendship Evangelism Action Response

List three people you are friendly with who are, to the best of your knowledge, not Christians:

1. _____

2. _____

3. _____

Your Action Response is threefold:

PRAY:

☐ Will you commit yourself to praying every day for the next week (month, or some time you determine) for these three friends?

PREPARE:

To get ready to share Christ with your friends, will you do any of the following?

☐ Read about evangelism

☐ Invite them to join a 'Just Looking', 'Youth Alpha' or other similar group.

☐ Join an evangelism training class

PURSUE:

To go after your friends, what actions will you take to start reaching out to them?

☐ Invite them to youth group

☐ Find out about their pastimes and interests

☐ Give them a phone call for a chat

☐ Invite them to your home, to build your friendship

GOLDEN OLDIES

MEETING AIM: This session introduces the challenge of serving the elderly of the community. Stereotypes, bad experiences and actual separation from old people can keep teenagers from reaching out to the aged, yet these are often the most responsive and needy people in the community. By seeing elderly people from God's perspective and by breaking down some of the barriers that exist between young and old, this session builds the foundation for potential long-term outreach to and relationships with the elderly.

WISE WORDS (10 mins)

In small groups, have the young people write down a collection of wise sayings or lessons that they have learned from the elderly people they know – grandparents, neighbours, or family friends. (Eg, 'Look after the pennies and the pounds will look after themselves'.)

TELLING TALES (10 mins)

Just about every young person knows the one or two favourite stories that his grandmother or grandfather may like to tell during every visit. Have your youngsters share some of these stories in small groups. Then discuss together why you think these stories might be so memorable or important to your grandparents.

WHEN I'M 64 (10 mins)

This exercise is designed to help young people to try to feel the pains and fears of the elderly. Try to maintain a fairly serious attitude in the group as you go through these, for too much humour will tend to foster mockery of the elderly rather than compassion for them. You could use the Beatles track 'When I'm 64' as background music.

Say: 'We want to try to imagine what it is like to be an elderly person. I am going to give you a phrase that describes the real world in which many older people live. Then I want you to offer your thoughts and feedback as to how you would feel if you were in their position.'

1. If my body was not functioning the way I wanted it to, I would feel...

2. If nobody from my family ever visited me, I would feel...

3. If people kept telling me I was in my "golden" years, I would feel...

4. If all my friends and my spouse had died, I would feel....

5. If I were really unsure as to where my money would come from, I would feel...

6. If every day I was reminded by my body that I am going to die soon, I would feel...

7. If I started forgetting things so much that I thought I was going crazy, I would feel...

8. If everything around me was changing so fast that I knew I could never keep up, I would feel...

9. If I went into a store and young kids laughed at me because of my looks, I would feel...

10. If no one ever called me on the phone, I would feel...

After this exercise, say: 'We really do not know everything about how old people think or feel, but we can understand why so many of them are fearful, lonely and frustrated. One of the solutions to their problems is understanding how God sees them, but they can understand best that God loves them as we show love to them.' A recent 'case study' from the newspaper that illustrates how elderly people feel about themselves can help reinforce your point here.

GOD AND OLD AGE (15 mins)

This exercise can be done in small groups or in one large group, as long as a few young people do not dominate the answers in the large group. Hand out copies of the sheet opposite, plus pens/pencils.

Start by saying: 'So that we can communicate God's love and concern to the old people in our lives, we must understand God's view of them.' Ask them to work through the Bible verses on the sheet which all relate to elderly people.

1. Proverbs 20:29 What is the difference between old men and young men? (Young men glory in physical strength, while old men are honoured by grey hair.) Why is grey hair an honour? (The people in the Old Testament saw grey hair as a sign of wisdom that has been accumulated with a long life.)

2. Psalm 37:25 What is the old psalmist's testimony? (In all his years, God had always been faithful to his people, the 'righteous'.) What can we learn from old people? (Those who follow Christ can tell us of how God has always taken care of them.)

3. Ephesians 6:2–3 (or Exodus 20:12) What is one of the rewards of obeying your parents? (A long life.) (Read also Proverbs 10:27.)

4. Matthew 25:35–36 What are two ways we serve the Lord by serving the elderly? (By caring for those who are lonely [the 'stranger'] and by visiting the sick.) As we care for the elderly, who are we caring for? (The Lord wants us to act towards them the same way as we would if we were serving him in person.)

5. James 1:27 What does God consider 'true religion'? (Visiting orphans and widows and staying free from worldly sins.) Why are orphans and widows so special to God? (Because they are the outcasts and the lonely that he is especially concerned about.)

Close this section by reading these verses:

'Is not wisdom found among the aged? Does not long life bring understanding?' (Job 12:12). 'Grey hair is a crown of splendour; it is attained by a righteous life' (Proverbs 16:31).

Then say: 'God considers old people very special because their long lives have helped them accumulate wisdom. We need to see them as people not only loved by God, but blessed by God with years of experience from which we can learn.'

YOU MAY FEEL OLD BUT... (15 mins)

Based on the Scripture study of this session, have your young people write a letter to elderly people at a nursing home or wardened accommodation entitled 'You May Feel Old But...'

If your group is larger than 10, break into groups of five or six. Give them some church letterhead and say: 'Just as you and I do, elderly people suffer from feelings of low self-esteem, thinking, 'Nobody likes me' or 'I wish I were dead.' God's message to these people, however, is quite different. He sees them as valuable, wise and special. But old people do not know God's view of them unless somebody tells them, and that is what we want to do.

'Using the scriptures we looked at earlier, write a letter to the folks at _____ [choose a nursing home in your community]. Explain to them that as teenagers you understand a little of the feelings they are going through, but that you want them to know what God thinks of them. Then summarise some of the lessons we learned from the Bible; you can quote verses if you like. When you have finished, sign your full name. Remember to write clearly.'

OLD TIME RELIGION (10 mins)

Invite an elderly member of your church to attend the youth group so they can share a testimony of their personal experience of God. Finish with a question and answer session where your young people can ask about what the advantages and disadvantages of being old are, what old people can give to the church, what it means to be old and yet a valued member of the church, etc.

OPTIONAL EXTRA

A visit to or service at a nursing home or wardened accommodation is especially appropriate as a response to this session. If you decide to do this, make sure you prepare the people you plan to visit (do not just 'drop by'). Prepare your young people for what they may see. Instruct them on how to care, to ask questions, and to listen. If it is near Christmas, one idea is to take your group to sing carols at a nursing home.

God and old age

Read the passages one at a time and try to answer the questions.

1) Proverbs 20:29

● What is the difference between old men and young men?

● Why do you think the Bible considers grey hair an honour?

2) Psalm 37:25

● What is the old psalmist's testimony?

● What can we learn from old people?

3) Ephesians 6:2–3 (or Exodus 20:12)

● What is one of the rewards of obeying your parents?

4) Matthew 25:35–36

● What are two ways we serve the Lord by serving the elderly?

● As we care for the elderly, who are we caring for?

5) James 1:27

● What does God consider 'true religion'?

● Why are orphans and widows so special to God?

ACROSS THE CULTURES

MEETING AIM: This session is designed to help your group start building bridges to those outside of their ethnic group. Prejudice, racism and bigotry are all enemies to the gospel and deter us from sharing the love of Christ with sincerity and effectiveness. This session will help identify the prejudices that we all have and then show how we can make new friends and begin to reach out to people from different ethnic groups and backgrounds.

WAS JESUS WHITE? (15 mins)

It is often observed that twentieth-century Britain has a very white, middle-class view of Jesus and God. Start your young people thinking by asking them to write a response to the statements on the sheet opposite. Hand out copies and pens and allow them five to eight minutes. Then get feedback and discussion. The key here is to try to find out how much your group link Christianity with the United Kingdom. In case you hadn't realised, Jesus would have had brown eyes, dark hair and deep olive coloured skin far from the blue-eyed, fair-haired image you often see in stained glass or picture books!

LET'S TALK (10–15 mins)

From your church or youth group, ask four or five adults or young people who come from ethnically identified groups (Black, Jewish, Bengali, Polish, Korean, etc) to take part in a panel discussion. Start the discussion with two or three questions of your own (samples below), and then open it up for the group to ask questions.

If you use adults, brief them beforehand so that their answers are geared to your group members. Encourage panel members to be honest and to offer suggestions as to how the church could be more sensitive.

You might begin with these questions:

1. How strongly linked do you feel to your ethnic heritage?

2. What do you feel like when your ethnic group is the topic of someone else's joke?

3. Do you feel that people at church are sensitive to your ethnic background?

4. Does your ethnic background affect at all the way you perceive God or relate to him?

5. How else does prejudice against your ethnic heritage manifest itself?

CAN OF QUESTIONS (15 mins)

Many scriptures, especially on the life of Jesus, demonstrate God's love for people of other ethnic or social groups. To encourage the group to listen to all of the following texts, tell them that after the scriptures have been read, a can will circulate containing questions they will be asked to answer.

Texts to be read:

1. Galatians 3:28
2. Luke 10:29–37
3. 2 Kings 5:1–14

These are some of the questions that you should include, but try writing some of your own which relate to your own local situation:

From Galatians 3:28:

1. Do all ethnic groups disappear in Christ?

2. Is everyone equal in Christ? Why?

3. Does the Bible say that sexual differences or social distinctions should be abolished? (You may want to explain the intense ethnic significance of being Gentile or Samaritan to the Jewish readers of the New Testament.)

From Luke 10:29–37:

4. Why does Jesus tell the story of the Good Samaritan?

5. Did the priest, Levite or Samaritan know the man who got robbed?

6. What does Jesus teach is the way we should treat 'neighbours' who we do not know or who might be ethnically different from us?

From 2 Kings 5:1–14:

7. Why was the King of Israel upset at the letter from the King of Syria?

8. What ethnic prejudices does Naaman demonstrate when Elisha gives the command?

9. Why is the story of Naaman a story of God's love for all people?

(Remind the young people that Naaman was a Syrian – the Syrians were often at war with the Jews.)

After the passages have been read, have the group close their Bibles. Pass the can around so that people get at least one question each (or, in the case of group studies, one question per group). Ask them to answer the question without opening the Bible. (If they do not know the answer, give them the Scripture reference on the question so they can look up the answer.)

AFRICAN BRAINTEASER (5 mins)

Ask the young people to get into groups of three. Give each small group a copy of the African Brainteaser sheet opposite and explain that they are going to enter the culture of East Africa for three minutes to try to work out this riddle!

(Answer: He takes the goat across and puts it on the other side. He returns for the cassava leaves and takes them across. On the return trip, he takes the goat back. He takes the leopard and leaves the goat. Then he returns for the goat.)

Someone is bound to ask you what a cassava is. It is a family of tropical plants with fleshy edible rootstocks which yield a nutritious starch.

GOING GREEK (1 min)

Explain that the words which we translate 'nations' in Matthew 28:19 are 'ta ethne'. Ask which English word is directly related to the Greek word for nations (ethnic). (Write ethne on a board/OHP to help the young people visualise it as the root of ethnic.) When we read Jesus' Great Commission, we should understand that he is concerned for every people group to come to have faith in him; this is one of our motivations for going outside of our own group to reach out to others. Explain that 'people group' doesn't just mean 'racial group', as within one small area even though everyone living there has the same racial background there can still be different people groups. Other factors such as income, education, regional accents, religion and age can divide people into different tribes, gangs or sub-groups.

COLOUR BLIND (5 mins)

Explain that according to the teaching of the Bible and the example of Jesus, Christians are supposed to be lovers of all people, regardless of their background. In our sinful world, however, this is hard to do. We all have a lot of growing to do in this respect, so consider three simple steps to help your growth:

Step One: Recognise the biblical examples. Jesus reached out to Samaritans and Gentiles – ethnic groups that his people, the Jews, would have hated. Elisha healed a Syrian; Ruth and Rahab (both Gentiles) were put by God in the line of the Messiah (Matthew 1:5); and Paul wrote that ethnic differences were to be laid aside by people who follow Christ.

Step Two: Repent of your bad attitudes. Maybe you need to ask people to forgive you for your racist or prejudiced attitudes. Perhaps you have some "enemies" who you need to start loving or praying for.

Step Three: Reach out to people who are different from you. Identify one or two people who you have stayed away from because of ethnic differences, and determine to start making friendships with those people.

LAST NAME GAME (15 mins)

This activity will take a fair amount of preparation, but it helps the young people develop a positive appreciation for cultures and people (who may live within your community).

Prepare five fictitious case studies of five teenagers. Three have parents who entered the UK in the 1960s from overseas (you choose where from). Two are white, but come from very different social backgrounds to the majority of the members of your youth group.

In groups, the young people are assigned the task of writing a fictitious cultural history for one of the teenagers (or all five). Some of the things you can encourage them to include are cultural distinctives such as:

● What distinctive language/dialect/accent does this person's parents have?
● What, if any, is the religion of his parents likely to be?
● How would he/she celebrate holidays (and what holidays does he/she celebrate)?
● What cultural distinctives does he/she adhere to which differ from the majority of people in our area?

● Does his/her cultural background affect his/her view of me? If so in what ways?
● Is this person glad they live in our community? Give reasons…

Then encourage your group to close their reports by completing this statement: 'When considering this person as a potential friend who I can get to know, learn from and share my faith with, I will need to remember to be sensitive to these cultural factors: … ' The answers may vary, but they should help sensitise your group to the fact that our cultural/

ethnic/societal backgrounds do affect us and the way we think.

N.B. This important section will only work well if you prepare thoroughly. Think through their likely comments, get advice and input from members of other cultural groups about what they think/how they would answer. Be prepared to deal with any outright racist or bigoted remarks, and don't let them throw you off balance!

WAS JESUS WHITE?

Write a short response to the statements below:

● **We in the Christian church are too often guilty of fostering the image of a white, middle-class God.**

....
....
....

● **Jesus was a white man.**

....
....
....

● **God shows special favour to the British.**

....
....
....

● **The normal way to worship God is the way we do it at our church.**

....
....
....

● **If Jesus walked the earth today, he would feel at home in our church.**

....
....
....

african brainteaser
A man has a leopard, a goat and a basket of cassava leaves that he needs to get across the river in his boat. He can only fit one item in his boat at a time, yet he knows that the goat will eat the leaves if left with them, and the leopard will eat the goat if it is not guarded. How does he get across the river?

HELPING THE HURTING

MEETING AIM: To teach that one of the key motives for evangelism is love. Jesus teaches that we should reach out to rather than avoid the person in desperate need. This session shows that people in the greatest need are often the most responsive to outreach.

BLIND EGG TORTURE (7 mins)
Ask for a volunteer. Once you get one, scatter a dozen eggs carefully onto the floor. Explain to the volunteer that they will need to walk blindfolded from one end of the room to the other, avoiding stepping onto and breaking the eggs.

While blindfolding the person have a couple of assistants remove the eggs and cover the floor with cornflakes. You will need some background music playing to cover the noise. This game is best played on a hard surface rather than carpet. Give the volunteer an egg to hold in their hand and explain that they must avoid getting tense otherwise they might crush the egg and get it all over their hand! (Unless you are very cruel, give the person an egg which you have blown the contents out of and filled with water instead.) The volunteer is usually a nervous wreck by the time they reach the other end of the room, especially if the rest of the group are screaming dire warnings! As the person reaches the end, congratulate them by shaking and squeezing their hand (the one with the blown egg in!). Give the brave volunteer a Cadbury's Creme Egg or some other appropriate prize for volunteering.

Then finish by saying: 'Have you ever thought what it must be like to have a disability like blindness, deafness or cerebral palsy?'

IMAGINE (15 mins)
Say: 'Most of us spend our time thinking about ourselves, but there are many people less fortunate than we are. We need to understand how they feel so we can care for them as we would like to be cared for if we were in their position.'

Hand out a pen and a copy of the worksheet opposite to every individual. Ask the young people to imagine themselves in various circumstances and then consider the top three problems they would confront each day and the primary way they would like others to care. You should set up a response chart as follows. You may want to add another couple of categories to the 'imagine you are...' column to identify needs in the area where you live.

Allow up to eight minutes for them to work through the sheet, then ask them to pair up with one other person to compare answers.

MOTHER TERESA SAYS... (5 mins)
Say: 'Nobel prize winner Mother Teresa worked among the poorest of the poor people in India. One of the operations of the Sisters of Mercy, which Mother Teresa founded, is a house for the terminally ill and dying. When asked why she did this, Mother Teresa simply said: "Because I see Christ in these people, and I want to comfort them as I would comfort him".'

Do you agree with her viewpoint?

OPINION POLL (10 mins)
Find out the opinions of your group towards people who are really hurting by asking them to give a response to the following questions. As you do this exercise, do not allow long answers that evolve into a debate. Have the young people share their answers and encourage them to differ without arguing.

1. Why do we hate it when someone begs us for money?

2. Why do we feel weird if we walk by a drunken man in the gutter?

3. Why are we so aware of people's clothing, especially if they are dressed poorly?

4. Why would your family feel awkward if a poor man knocked at your door and asked if he could stay the night?

5. Why do people ignore others who are crying out for help?

6. Why do we stare at people with physical handicaps?

7. Why do poor people stay poor rather than just going out to get a job?

8. Why don't rich people simply give their extra money to the poor to relieve their suffering?

9. Why do people sometimes cross the street when they see a visually impaired person coming towards them with either a walking stick or a guide dog?

10. Why does it sometimes irritate us when someone calls us for help in an emergency?

THE BIG QUESTION (3–5 mins)
Say: 'There are thousands of poor and homeless people in our country and in our world. Millions go without food, and tens of millions are not adequately dressed. We cannot change everything all at once, but we can change some things. But before we think about changing anything, we need to know why we do what we do. So, here is the big question: What is our number one reason for seeking to help or serve the poor and destitute?' (Record answers on a chalkboard or overhead projector.)

You may get various answers here, ranging from 'To serve Jesus' to 'Because we have so much'. Say: 'There are many good reasons to help the hurting. The Bible says: we serve these people because by serving them we are (in a mysterious way) serving Jesus himself. Let's read about this.'

Read (in the whole group) Matthew 25:31–46.

SHEEP OR GOAT? (20 mins)
Divide your group into smaller groups of at least five. Ask them to reread the passage and then fulfill one of these assignments.

If groups are small, tell the young people they must play multiple parts. You can help them by giving them construction paper on which to write the titles of the different needy people named in the passage to use as labels.

Assignment 1: Act out the passage.

Assignment 2: Write an obituary which announces the earthly death of one whom Jesus would label a 'sheep'.

Assignment 3: Write an obituary which announces the earthly death of one whom Jesus would call a 'goat'.

Assignment 4: Make a list of all the actions that Jesus mentions and try to give a modern-day equivalent of what you (or your group) could do to serve Jesus.

Assignment 5: Write a complaint letter from one of the 'goats' which defends the reasons why he thinks he should get to go to heaven, and then write Jesus' response.

MOTIVATION FOR MISSION (8 mins)
Say: 'The comments of Jesus in this chapter are very strong, and taken by themselves they may cause us to start wondering, "Am I a Christian? I've never visited a prisoner." On the other hand, we may gain a false confidence and say, "I help poor people all the time; I must be on my way to heaven for sure".'

The passage in Matthew 25 is not to be taken by itself. We must keep it in the overall context of Scripture. In the context of the whole Bible, Matthew 25 is not a teaching of Jesus on the basis of salvation. Instead, it is a teaching of Jesus on how those who are saved really act. From it, we must remember two big lessons:

1. The primary motivation for service to others must be to serve Jesus. If we serve him, we can know that he takes notice and will reward such behaviour in heaven.

2. Jesus is saying that the lifestyle of a true believer in him is characterised by concern for the 'down-and-out' person – the hungry, lonely, ill-clothed or destitute. As his followers, we must make choices to care for those in great need.

Conclude by asking the group to fill in this statement and apply it this week.

'Based on what Matthew 25 teaches, this week I am going to serve Jesus in this way:_____'

A postcard that young people can carry with them for the week in their pockets or wallets is ideal.

imagine...

Imagine you are....	Your top three concerns would be:	You would like someone to care for you by:
1. Confined to a wheelchair		
2. Blind		
3. Desperately poor		
4. Living on the streets		
5. Deaf		
6. Hungry (have not eaten in four days)		
7. Lonely (no friends)		
8. Unemployed		

WORLD-CLASS PRAYER

MEETING AIM: To show the need to be world-minded – to be open to the concerns of the whole world, not locked into our own little world.

CATEGORIES (8 mins)

Use a game of categories to introduce the theme of prayer for the world. Hand out an A5 sheet of paper and a pen to every member of your group and ask them to write in capital letters the word 'PRAY' down the left-hand side of the page. They then have to come up with a word beside each letter according to your instructions. The word should ideally be one no one else in the group writes down. So, for instance, if you asked them to write down a boy's name starting with 'P' they could write down 'Peter' but they risk lots of others writing that name too. A more unusual name like 'Pip' might be better. On the other hand, everyone might avoid the common names, so you never know!

The scoring system works like this: At the end of the game everyone in turn calls out the word they have chosen, If they are the only person who chose a particular word, they score 10 points; if one other person also chose that word they both score nine; if three did, they each score eight. If a total of 10 or more chose that same word they all score just one point. If they couldn't come up with a word, they don't score anything.

Allow just 60 seconds thinking time for each letter. The categories are:

P a type of food (eg, peanuts)
R an overseas city (eg, Rome)
A a country (eg, Austria)
Y a girls name (eg, Yvonne)

The winner is the person with the most points. Categories is a useful game which can be used to introduce virtually any topic.

WORLD-CLASS CHRISTIAN (5–10 mins)

Ask the young people to form groups of two or three, then hand out copies of the sheet opposite and a pen to each group. They also need a Bible. Say: 'The Bible is full of examples of the ways Christians should respond to the needs of the world. How much do you know about practical "world Christian" living?' Allow about eight minutes, then read out the answers.

(Answers: 1b, 2c, 3a, 4b, 5b.)

MISSIONARY TALE (10 mins)

If possible, have a missionary who is on furlough share a testimony of how God directed them to their particular mission location. Ask the missionary to share how they came to be a missionary. If you do this, make sure you brief them on your group and offer tips on talking to young people.

NEWSPAPER SEARCH (15 mins)

Have a pile of recent daily newspapers and as many pairs of scissors as you can find. Then ask the young people to go through the pile of newspaper and cut out every article they can find related to international affairs. If you remove beforehand sections like the sports, movie ads, or the cartoon page you will more easily keep your young people from getting off track. (N.B. The tabloid papers usually have less coverage of international affairs so make sure there are plenty of broadsheet papers.)

After about six minutes of cutting, ask the young people to get together to share what they have found with three or four others. Chances are, one or two international events will dominate the news stories. Ask them to concentrate on the one or two countries that have been most in the news recently.

When the young people have decided which countries they will focus on, ask them to list what they think would be the prayer concerns for missionaries and national Christians in those countries. After completing this task, have the group share their answers.

PRAYER POWER (20 mins)

Start by saying: 'We often wonder where we fit into God's worldwide concern, especially in day-to-day experience. One of the ways in which we can make missions a part of our day-to-day growth as Christians is prayer.'

Divide the group into groups of three or four. Then assign each group three verses related to prayer. Each group then looks up the verses and answers these questions:

1. What promise or command does God give us about prayer? 2. How should these verses change our thinking about prayer? 3. In what ways should these verses apply to our prayers for the world or for missionaries?

Some sample verses you can choose from are: Philippians 4:19; Ephesians 3:20–21; Jeremiah 33:3; Mark 9:23; Isaiah 65:24; John 16:24; Philippians 4:6–7; James 5:13–16 ; Colossians 4:2–4; Matthew 9:36–38; Ephesians 6:18–20; 1 Timothy 2:1–4.

After each group has answered the questions, have them share their answers for the benefit of the whole group. (Writing their answers on an overhead transparency can help the whole group see the answers.)

TALK-TO (10 mins)

Say: 'On a daily basis, the main way that we can be involved around the world is through our prayers.

'Imagine for a moment that the Prime Minister called you on the phone and asked you to 10 Downing Street to consult with him about foreign affairs. Do you think you would

find the time to go and meet with him? I know that I would, not because I know that much about foreign affairs, but because I know that the Prime Minister has great influence in world events. This is the privilege that we have every day if we are Christians. God, the all-powerful ruler of the universe, invites us to pray, to consult with him, about world events. We need to take him up on this invitation for at least two reasons.

'First, like the boy who offered his loaves and fishes, we can see God do a mighty work through our little offering, our prayers. Through our prayers, God will act and, as a result, we play a part in influencing world history.

'Second, on a more personal level, praying about the needs of the world will change us. As we start praying for world situations – like hunger or earthquake, or hopelessness or wars – we begin to get a better perspective on our own lives. Maybe our problems are just not that big after all. As we learn to trust God with the big issues of our world, we can also trust him with our personal concerns.'

Close in prayer. Remind your group about the countries or areas of the world (Newspaper Search) that have been especially turbulent recently. Encourage the young people, now that they know some of God's commands and promises related to prayer, to spend some time in their groups praying specifically for Christians and Christian missionaries in these countries.

Alternatively, you could play a video clip recorded from last night's TV news bulletin which focuses on a particularly urgent need in a foreign country, and use that as a prayer prompt.

If your young people find it hard to pray out loud, be creative about getting them to pray. Try asking them to write down a prayer and then read it out...

OPTIONAL EXTRAS

Option 1 Sharing selections out of one of the many biographies of either Hudson Taylor or George Mueller can be excellent for stimulating excitement about the ways in which God answers prayers.

Option 2 This is perhaps the best session to introduce a 'Missions Adoption' programme in which your youth group 'adopts' a foreign missionary. Prayer cards, letters and reports from this missionary can inspire your young people to pray and – through the adopted missionary – to have an impact on some other part of the world. (Good adoption programmes usually begin with prayer but soon evolve into correspondence, missionary visits and gifts from the youth group to the missionary you have adopted.)

world-class Christians

1. The first priority of Christians is to:
a. go to be missionaries;
b. give themselves to God;
c. make sure their own needs are met.
(See 2 Corinthians 8:5)

2. God promises a day when:
a. everybody will be Christians;
b. all the poor will overtake the rich;
c. everyone will realise who God is.
(See Habakkuk 2:14)

3. One example of God using a little gift to do a great work is:
a. the story of the boy's loaves and fishes;
b. the story of the mustard seed;
c. the story of the Good Samaritan;
(See John 6:5–14)

4. God prefers:
a. religious services;
b. shared bread;
c. frequent fasting;
(See Isaiah 58:5–7)

5. When a Christian commits themselves to helping someone, they should:
a. give no matter what;
b. give as generously as we would to Jesus;
c. give when things are going well for us.
(See 2 Corinthians 9:7)

WORLD-CLASS COMPASSION

MEETING AIM: The world's needs are so great that we can never care for every need or every person. This session focuses on the need to balance heart-felt compassion with practical involvement, so that we become neither apathetic nor overwhelmed by it all.

JUST IMAGINE IF... (5 mins)

Start by asking your group to imagine what they would have to do to move from their country to any one of the world's poorest countries, like Paraguay, Somalia, Haiti, Chad or Afghanistan. Can they imagine it? Ask the following questions about how they would live.

1. Your home would be approximately as large as a British:
a) house b) garage c) toolshed d) kennel.

2. Which of the following furniture would you probably have?
a) a table, chairs, bed, one chest b) a table, one chair, a few blankets c) a table, no chairs, a bed and no chest d) a table, chairs, stove, bed and chest.

3. To eat you'd probably have:
a) dried meat and a few vegetables b) a little flour, salt and sugar, mouldy potatoes, dried beans and onions c) only rice d) dried meat, vegetables, and powered milk.

4. You would get water from:
a) a tap in your yard b) the village well c) a river.

5. You would probably own:
a) electric lights b) a pet dog c) a saw d) no tools or pets.

6. You would get information from:
a) magazines b) your radio c) your TV d) the village radio.

7. When you got sick, you would go to:
a) the doctor down the street b) a clinic ten miles away, run by a midwife c) the hospital in the next town d) heaven.

8. Your life expectancy would probably be:
a) about the same as now b) ten years less c) 25 – 30 years less d) 40 – 50 years less.

(ANSWERS: 1c, 2b, 3b, 4b, 5d, 6d, 7b, 8c.)

(Taken from Hunger: Understanding the Crisis through Games, Dramas & Songs, by Patricia Houck Sprinkle, © John Knox Press. Used by permission.)

Close the quiz by saying: 'The answers show us that we have a very tough time identifying with the poorest people in our world. Nevertheless, we must make a choice to care for them. The Bible calls this choice compassion.

I DON'T CARE (10 mins)

This can be done as a short, off-the-cuff sketch with yourself and one other person, or even better you could ask two young people from your group who like drama to rehearse this beforehand and perform it to the group.

A: 'I see that there was another earthquake in South America today.'
B: 'Uh-huh' [a half-hearted grunt that says, 'So what!'].
A: 'And did you know that a tidal wave is expected in Indonesia?'
B: 'No [perturbed], I guess I didn't know that.'
A: 'It's also a fact that dozens of people will die of hunger in just the time we have this conversation.'
B: 'So what do you want me to do?'
A: 'What about this then…there are over 2 billion people who don't know anything about Jesus.'
B: 'Why are you telling me this?'
A: 'To make you care.'
B: 'Care? How can I care? Anyway, I can't be bothered. I have enough problems of my own.'
A: 'But don't you realise that today in Burkina Faso…'
B: [Interrupts] 'But I don't care about Burkina Faso' [walks out angrily.]

After the person exits, ask the group to discuss their own feelings of frustration related to missions. You may find out that a lot of them can relate to 'B' and have adopted an 'I don't care' attitude because the world's need seems too vast. Or maybe it is because they have become desensitised to people's suffering and need, with so many famines, wars, refugees and other problems on TV.

WHAT DOES IT MEAN? (2 mins)

Explain that the Greek word which we translate 'compassion' (see Matthew 9:36–38 for an example) – is actually related to the word for intestines. In graphic terms, the word means that the one who is 'moved with compassion' is actually so affected by what he sees or knows that his 'guts' hurt or he becomes nauseated.

RANGES OF RESPONSE (15 mins)

Say: 'The Bible gives examples in which people were confronted with a need or opportunity and they responded.' Hand out pens and copies of the Bible study opposite. Either assign them to small groups or get them to work as individuals. Each group/person will need access to a New Testament. (Potential answers are in brackets)

After the chart is completed, ask the small groups: As we look at the great needs around the world, how will we respond? Will we be like any of these examples? Which of the motivations and responses do you think God wants us to have? Allow time for feedback to these questions.

PRACTICAL POINTERS (10 mins)

Say: 'We all know the frustration of hearing about needs and opportunities around the world and feeling powerless to respond. If we continue to develop this sense of helplessness, we can become apathetic.

There are practical ways to maintain compassion and to keep from apathy.

'First, we can start caring about the people right around us. We may not be able to tell a tribal person in Indonesia about Jesus, but we can tell our friends (and they may not know about Jesus' love either!).

'Second, we can pray, because this puts us in touch with the One in charge, God. We cannot care for the whole world, but we can stay in touch with the God who does. Through this contact, we can find out where we fit intohHis worldwide plan.

'Finally, we can get started learning about the world. One way to do this is to develop the habit of knowing everything about somewhere and something about everywhere.'

EVERYTHING ABOUT SOMEWHERE (10 mins)

Explain this exercise as a way to start maintaining a practical handle on world concerns. The idea is that the group will commit themselves to learning 'something about everywhere' (like where Burkina Faso is) and 'everything about somewhere'. The focus of the closing portion of this session is the latter. A world map or a globe is a must for this exercise.

Encourage your group to pick a place or country in the world. This becomes their 'somewhere'. Then explain that this area of interest can become a topic of prayer, reading and research. Their 'somewhere' becomes a special area or people or country for which they can have compassion by really getting interested and involved. Before asking the group to pick their 'somewhere', tell them about a particular place or people for whom you are praying. Tell the group how you are learning about the place (National Geographic, the newspaper, etc,) and what you hope to do in terms of prayer for missions and compassion for that specific concern. Your personal enthusiasm and example are the most important ingredients for making this work.

After the group have picked a 'somewhere', close with a time of prayer for these places or people.

Check out *Operation World: A Handbook for World Intercession* (Patrick J. Johnstone, OM). This is an excellent country-by-country compilation of information about the Christian church around the world.

Ranges of Response

Scripture verses	People involved	Response	Motivation for the response?
1. Luke 9:49–50	(Jesus, disciples, man preaching in Jesus' name)	(Disciples wanted to forbid him)	(Jealousy?)
2. Luke 9:51–56	(Jesus, disciples, Samaritans)	(Disciples wanted to call down fire on them)	(Anger, hatred, revenge)
3. Romans 5:8	(God, Jesus, us)	(In spite of our sins, God sent Jesus)	(Love)
4. Acts 16:9–10	(Paul, Macedonians)	(He responded to the dream/call for help)	(Love, desire to obey God)
5. Luke 14:16–20	(Man throwing a party and invitees)	(They were too busy to come)	(Too busy)
6. Matthew 9:36–39	(Jesus, troubled people)	(Prayer)	(Compassion)

SECTION 5
HOT ISSUES

These 'hot issues' meeting plans will work just as well in a one-off format as a term-long series. Either way they are sure to create lively debate, discussion and thinking over subjects which matter to young people. As well as listening to each other I trust these meetings will also help your young people into a better understanding of what Scripture says on these vital subjects. In short, as well as generating heat these meetings are designed to shed light.

1. POPULARITY
What makes a person popular? Dangers of courting popularity. Biblical examples of people who were popular without rejecting godly values.

2. GRUDGES
Holding grudges is incompatible with being a Christian. Ways to resolve conflicts and ongoing grudge situations.

3. GOSSIP
What is gossip? This session highlights its destructiveness and suggests strategies to overcome talking too much.

4. EXAM PRESSURE
Coping with revision and the expectations of others. How God can help us cope with stressful situations.

5. ALCOHOL
What does the Bible say about alcohol and peer pressure to drink?

6. CONSEQUENCES
A person reaps what they sow. What is your life likely to produce?

7. SEXISM
To explore the subject of sexism and give young people a greater understanding of the issues involved.

8. ABSOLUTES
In our relativistic culture, Scripture teaches that God has provided non-negotiable principles.

9. ANIMAL RIGHTS
Do animals have equal rights to people?

10. I'LL BE THERE FOR YOU
Ways to support others through crisis.

POPULARITY

MEETING AIM: To help people understand why popularity is so important to all of us; to show the dangers of courting popularity; to make it clear that Christians should be attractive, but won't always be popular.

Look out for possible pastoral problems which may surface – those in the group who find acceptance a problem (and that may include some surprisingly confident-seeming young people!) may find this subject stirs emotions which you need to address in a personal chat later.

INTRODUCTION (10 mins)

Before the meeting, hang up around the room 10 numbered photographs (five male, five female) of people unknown to the group (newspaper photos of non-celebrities would do). Photocopy the 10 boxes on the sheet opposite which bear the names of personal qualities and the 10 'situation' cards. Then cut them into 20 cards and hang or stick these up around the room also.

Ask the group to go around and pick out:
(a) which two faces they find most attractive;
(b) which four qualities they'd most like those people to possess;
(c) which four 'situation cards' they would like to be true of those people.

Discuss the results.

Then say: 'We've been exploring just what it is that makes others attractive to us. When we meet new people, we warm to some of them, and we're not so interested in others. We would all like to be people who get others excited. Do these results give a fair picture of where popularity comes from?'

I WANT TO BE LOVED BY YOU (7 mins)

Why do we all want to be popular? Draw a diagram of a pyramid with five layers.

Say: 'A few years ago, psychologist Abraham Maslow taught that we all have basic needs. The base of the pyramid is our PHYSICAL NEEDS – food, clothing and shelter. Once these needs are met, we have SECURITY needs (you may be well fed and warm, but you need to feel safe). Once these are met, we need ESTEEM – a group of people who like us. Then there's LOVE, and finally SELF-ACTUALISATION, which means reaching our full potential as a human being.

'So it's hard to feel loved, or to reach our peak, unless we feel esteemed first. Humans weren't made to be alone; they need the group.'

If you can find it, play Paul Simon's old song *I am an island* (or distribute copies of the words), and discuss where they think the singer gets it wrong.

THE TROUBLE WITH ME (8 mins)

Now give everyone a pen, and a piece of paper containing two half-sentences: 'I would be more popular if…' and 'The best things I have going for me are…'

Ask them to think about the results we came up with earlier, and then fill in the rest of the sentences. Stress that this exercise is for their eyes only. Nobody else, not even you, will look at the results.

After giving enough time for completion, ask: 'Are Christians supposed to be popular or not?' Let them discuss the question for a few minutes, then make two points: (a) Christians should be attractive to others (Acts 2:47; Matthew 5:16; Titus 3:2–8); (b) for the sake of the gospel, Christians won't always be liked (1 John 3:13; Matthew 10:34). So we have to be careful that we really are good people to know, but we shouldn't be so keen for popularity that we'll sacrifice anything to get it.

WHEN IT GOES WRONG (10 mins)

In four small groups, look at one of these case studies each.

BEN desperately wants to be popular. He is slightly younger than the rest of his group of friends, and he feels much less experienced and mature. He knows that some of the others laugh about him behind his back, but he can't resist talking big, pretending to be more adult than he really is, and trying to stay included in everything. Sometimes he feels angry and wonders why he's bothering. But something just drives him on.

JO has fallen out with her best friend over something completely trivial. Now she feels miserable. She doesn't think it was all her fault, but she has tried to apologise anyway; but it isn't working. What's worse, the other girls in her group have started to treat her like a bad smell. She feels completely isolated and can't think what to do.

ED would love to be the life and soul of the party, the centre of attention and approval, but he knows it will never happen. He just isn't very interesting, very handsome, very funny or very good at anything. He can never think of anything to say when he gets into a conversation. It isn't that people dislike him or treat him badly; it's just that they never seem to notice he's there. And honestly Ed can't blame them. Why should they?

MIRANDA has loads and loads of friends. She is flamboyant, attractive, dynamic and fun. But because she spends her life in a whirl of activity, dashing from group to group, she never develops very deep relationships with anyone. And sometimes, lying in bed at night, she wonders if anybody really does like her or even understand her properly. But nobody would ever guess she feels this way.

Ask the group:

(a) What advice could you give to this person?
(b) Does this case study teach you anything about popularity?

Compare results, and ask people to think silently for themselves: Which of these case studies is most like me?

LOVE ME, LOVE MY FRIENDS (10 mins)

Say: 'There are dangers in seeking popularity. The book of Proverbs was written to guide young people as they grew up, and it contains lots of warnings.'

Get each small group to read Proverbs 1:10–19 and answer these questions:
(a) Why can it be dangerous to seek popularity?
(b) What's more important than popularity?
(c) Can you think of a modern-day parallel to the situation described here?

(If your group enjoy drama, and time allows, they could turn their answer to (c) into an instant sketch…)

Discuss for a few minutes: what are the biggest temptations that young people can be led into by seeking popularity? (under-age clubbing, drug-taking, treating others badly, shoplifting…)

BALANCING ACT (10 mins)

Now look at some young people who got it right. Get them to read Daniel 1:1–17 (perhaps you may need to explain a bit of the background history first), and then report on:
● Three pressures that Daniel and his friends were under
● Three signs that they became popular
● Why they refused to go along with the crowd, just to be popular
● Three results of the way they behaved.

Say: 'Daniel and his friends were obviously in a pretty extreme situation. But if they could cope with so much pressure and still remain faithful to God without losing their popularity with others, then maybe we can do the same. Their secret was that they trusted God to sort it out for them. They didn't try to make it all happen by themselves.'

FINALLY (5 mins)

Put your results together, and recap on all the main lessons you've learned from this session. Close in prayer, asking God to make us attractive people, but not so desperate for popularity that we let him down. Pray for those who don't feel included, and ask God to show us how we can help one another to gain confidence and esteem, and grow more and more into a true sense of family.

PERSONAL QUALITY Imagination	PERSONAL QUALITY Calm	SITUATIONS Widely read	SITUATIONS Artistically gifted
PERSONAL QUALITY Sense of humour	PERSONAL QUALITY Charm	SITUATIONS Many friends	SITUATIONS Great cook
PERSONAL QUALITY Enthusiasm	PERSONAL QUALITY Unpredictability	SITUATIONS Rich background of experience	SITUATIONS Influential in high places
PERSONAL QUALITY Gentleness	PERSONAL QUALITY Neatness	SITUATIONS Physically stunning	SITUATIONS Always available
PERSONAL QUALITY Kindness	PERSONAL QUALITY Wisdom	SITUATIONS Extremely wealthy	SITUATIONS Personally brave

GRUDGES

MEETING AIM: To show that holding grudges is incompatible with being a Christian, and to suggest ways of resolving conflicts.

This meeting plan is aimed at a group that already has some commitment. If possible, don't tell them in advance what the meeting's theme is to be; the whole thing depends on their honesty in filling in the 'Personal Hit List' at the start.

The last section needs careful handling, since it introduces personal issues which may run very deep. Keep a look-out for individuals who may need a personal chat afterwards. If you know of feuds or dislikes existing within the group at the moment, be very careful not to make people feel that you are singling them out for disapproval. The aim is not to condemn, but to help people see for themselves what standard of behaviour God expects from us.

UNFORGETTABLE, THAT'S WHAT YOU ARE (10 mins)

Divide into small groups and give each group one of the profiles from the sheet opposite, which portrays a fictional character. In each case, the profile contains one 'nasty' fact which might cause a bad relationship with the person described. Ask each group to decide which of these details would be the last thing you'd forget about this person. Then compare results.

Most groups will pick out the 'grudge' detail. Ask why this is? Why do we have such long memories when people let us down?

Issue everybody with a sheet divided into four columns, headed 'Personal Hit List'. Ask them to write in the first column the names of the three people they most intensely dislike in the world. Leave the rest of the sheet blank meanwhile.

WE'RE ONLY HUMAN (7 mins)

Point out that holding grudges is a universal human trait. Before communism came to Albania, there were bitter 'blood feuds' between families which went on for generations. In the decades of repression, these feuds disappeared, but they hadn't been forgotten. As soon as freedom came to Albania, the blood feuds started up again. Killings in Bosnia, Rwanda and Zaire are all because people have long memories of disagreements.

Test your group's memory of Bible stories. What was the 'grudge' story connected with these figures: Saul and David? Paul and Barnabas? Joseph and his brothers? Haman and Mordecai? Shimei and David? Absalom and Amnon? (If they haven't a clue about the last two, tell the stories from 2 Samuel 16 and 19, and 2 Samuel 13. Ask: 'Who behaved badly and who behaved well in these incidents?')

TRACING IT BACK (10 mins)

Where do grudges come from? In small groups, ask them to share one of the stories on their 'Hit List', answering these questions:

● How did the bad feeling start?
● What made it worse?
● Who was to blame for what happened?
● What's the state of affairs now?

After hearing all the stories, the group should choose one to present as a case study to the other groups (maybe through role-play, if they feel confident enough).

Watch all the playlets, and ask:
● What do we learn from this about how grudges start?
● What helps to keep them growing?

(Don't ask people to suggest solutions at this stage. For the moment, we're just examining causes.)

PICK A FIGHT (10 mins)

Now pair each small group up with another one. Tell them they have to find something to quarrel about. Let them talk, fall out and argue for about four minutes. Then call a halt and ask: 'How difficult did you find it to disagree?' The answer is always 'not at all'!

Ask: 'How did you manage to quarrel?' Point out that it's usually something small and trivial to begin with but it rapidly becomes very important indeed. The more you keep arguing, the more convinced you become that you are right!

(If you have time, a little exercise which demonstrates this is to ask people to pick a partner and choose a colour, then spend three minutes arguing with their partner, trying to show that their colour is 'better' than the other person's. Most people start this exercise realising how silly and pointless it is, but amazingly, after three minutes, most have argued themselves into believing that there really is something superior about their chosen colour!)

Now for something more difficult. Select two group members from each 'conflict situation' to go into another one and act as mediator. They have four minutes to sort it out and bring reconciliation.

Ask: 'How easy was that?' The inevitable answer is that it was much more difficult. Grudges are easy to get into but hard to escape from. Discuss what techniques the mediators used. What worked and what didn't? Then say that it's time to see what the Bible says about escaping from grudge situations.

BIBLE STUDY (13 mins)

In small groups, look at these passages and questions. (If your members aren't quick at finding Bible passages, give each sub-group one question each.)

● What's dangerous about holding grudges? (Acts 15:39; Hebrews 12:15; James 3:8–10)
● Why shouldn't we hold grudges? (Philippians 2:1–2; 1 Corinthians 10:32; 1 Peter 3:21-23)
● What can we do to avoid them? (Philippians 2:3–4; Matthew 18:15; Ephesians 4:26; James 1:19–21; Matthew 5:43–45)

Compare answers and summarise:
● If we're Christians, we should look like Jesus – and forgive like Jesus too.
● Holding grudges destroys us bit by bit; unresolved disagreements poison our lives.
● We need to deal with our anger, and act in love towards those who treat us badly.

If time allows, tell the story of the unforgiving servant (Matthew 18:21–35). Christians have been forgiven so much; they should be the first to forgive trifling offences and wrongs done by others. When we're annoyed with somebody, we should try to focus not on what they've done to us, but on what Jesus has already forgiven us for.

THIS MEANS YOU (10 mins)

Now ask them to look back at their 'Personal Hit List'. There are three blank columns next to each name. Ask them to write in these columns three loving things they could do for the person concerned – things which will help them to change their own feelings, and perhaps defuse any grudges which are building up. Give plenty of time for them to think this through, and perhaps pray about it personally. (In some groups, it may be appropriate to share results here; others will want to keep it private.)

Then finish in prayer, asking God to give the group courage to do some of the things they have come up with, and to use this coming week to grow more into the likeness of Jesus as they forgive others and restore broken relationships.

PROFILES:

Name:	Andy
Age:	17
Favourite band:	Oasis
Achievements:	won a trip to America in a local radio contest
Family:	two younger sisters
Peculiarities:	slight lisp
Good at:	computer graphics, drawing cartoons
Past record:	stole your girlfriend a year ago

Name:	Fiona
Age:	13
Favourite band:	Eternal
Achievements:	county gymnast, trials for England
Family:	parents divorced, no brothers or sisters
Peculiarities:	very bossy, a natural leader
Good at:	maths, baking cakes
Past record:	has owed you five pounds for the last year and still hasn't paid up

Name:	Gareth
Age:	15
Favourite band:	Louise
Achievements:	golf handicap of seven
Family:	one older brother
Peculiarities:	only drinks water
Good at:	mending broken golf equipment
Past record:	a year ago he promised to take you to his dad's golf club for a game but never did

Name:	Marie
Age:	16
Favourite band:	Radiohead
Achievements:	raised £300 single-handed for Comic Relief last year
Family:	parents separated, no brothers or sisters
Peculiarities:	double jointed in her fingers and toes
Good at:	cooking, rollerblading
Past record:	a year ago she daubed a message in the toilets at school that you were gay

GOSSIP

MEETING AIM: Gossip seems to pervade every part of our culture. There are programmes on TV and articles in magazines and newspapers which only consist of juicy titbits about the rich and famous. As young people grow older they begin to confide in other people (mainly friends from their peer group) instead of close family. As they become more independent these friendships become more important. But in our gossip-filled world the culture encourages people to blab about confidences. This session identifies what gossip is, highlights its destructiveness and suggests strategies to overcome talking too much.

WHAT IS GOSSIP? (5 mins)

Ask the group to define the word 'gossip' and write down their suggestions on a whiteboard or OHP. Look up the word in a dictionary beforehand. The combination of their ideas, plus you filling in any holes with your dictionary definition, should result in a full description.

Then say: 'Gossip can often lead to "slander" and "libel". The dictionary describes slander as "a false or malicious report which defames" – that is it takes away or destroys a good reputation – "to speak evil of". Libel is a written or spoken accusation which defames – that is destroys a reputation. Sometimes people who believe they have suffered from slander and libel resort to the law in order to extract a withdrawal and/or an apology, and to be cleared publicly of the libellous accusation. Sometimes the high legal costs and a claim for damages means the person who committed libel (especially if it is a newspaper or magazine) loses a lot of money.

'That said, most gossip is not exactly libellous; instead it is tittle-tattle, eroding a reputation in a minor way rather than a major full-blown attack on a person.'

GOSSIP HUNT (10 mins)

Collect a pile of teen magazines and tabloid newspapers beforehand. Put them in the middle of the room and then ask the group to dive in and carefully tear out stories and photo captions which they think are based on gossip. Allow them about five minutes to sift through the pile (you may need to encourage them not to get side-tracked by what they see and read).

Get them to report back on what they have found – you may find there are one or two current 'gossipy' news stories from the papers.

Identify phrases used in the media – on TV, in papers, magazines, etc – which basically mean 'This is a bit of juicy gossip'. Here are a few examples:

...and now Naomi Campbell has been spotted on a date with...

...it sounds horrible, but apparently it's true...

...news is that apparently the singer collapsed backstage. Insiders claim that he was drunk...

Ask: 'Why do papers and magazines contain so much that is based on gossip?' (Because they think their readers are interested in reading gossip.)

CHINESE WHISPERS (3 mins)

Get the whole group to form one line. (A line should have a minimum of eight people and preferably up to a maximum of 15 people. If you have more, form two or more lines.)

Tell them that you are going to whisper something to the head of the line, who in turn will whisper it to the next person and so on, until the message gets to the end of the line. Emphasise that it is important to whisper the message so that only the next person hears it. If the person doesn't hear the message properly, they can ask for it to be repeated, but only once! When the last person receives the message ask them to write it down or call it out. Then compare it to the original message. This usually raises a good laugh, as most times the original message has been corrupted and changed considerably. An example of an original message is given below. If you make up your own, ensure that it has at least 30 words.

Make the point that with each telling, a piece of gossip can change, become distorted and even more inaccurate than the original gossip. This shows how gossip is inaccurate, as well as potentially damaging.

My brother Jim saw Wesley and Sandy last night. They were leaving the fish and chip shop holding hands. If they're still going out with each other next week I reckon they'll be dancing together at the school end of term party. Do you?

TV GOSSIPS (10 mins)

Ask the group to identify characters from TV soaps who are gossips. You may like to video some soaps during the previous weeks and then show some clipped examples of gossip (there is usually no shortage of examples!).

Then ask the following questions:
● What sort of things do these characters gossip about? (Relationships, people who are in trouble/have made mistakes, unflattering comments about a persons appearance or lifestyle etc).
● Are they popular or unpopular characters within the soap? (Usually they are unpopular. Make the point that gossips are usually despised and disliked by people behind the gossip's back.)
● Why do these characters gossip? (Because they don't have much of a life themselves, out

of spite/for revenge, boredom, because they enjoy inflicting pain on others.)
● Do these characters enjoy gossiping? Why? (A way to socialise with people who might otherwise not talk to them, having information others want to know imparts a sense of power, etc.)

POSTER POWER (10–12 mins)

Say: 'During World War II the British people were encouraged not to talk about what they or their relatives and neighbours were doing for the war effort. For example, if a woman had a son who was a sailor on board a warship and he knew his boat was about to sail, she should not tell others that fact. The British government was worried that this sort of information could be picked up by German agents in Britain and then used to help the enemy plan their strategy. A whole series of posters were produced with headlines like "Careless talk costs lives" and "Loose lips sink ships". Although our country is not at war with a foreign nation, gossip can still be a destructive force.'

Ask the young people to form groups of twos or threes. Hand out A3 sheets of paper and pens, or alternatively blank acetates and OHP pens, and ask the groups to design posters which could be used to encourage people not to gossip. The posters can include visual images, but all should also include phrases which will help people to see how negative and destructive gossip can be. Allow up to eight minutes for this exercise and then ask each group to feed back their poster.

GOD AND GOSSIP (10–15 mins)

'The majority of the Old Testament book of Proverbs was written by Solomon, who was given extra wisdom by God. He is credited with having 'spoken' around 3,000 proverbs (1 Kings 4:32). Check out these verses from Proverbs, then try to summarise in a few words what the message is – eg 10:18–19: (gossips are fools, those who keep quiet are wise).'

(This exercise can be undertaken in small groups, or all together orally and written down on paper, followed by a feedback session. You decide what is best for your group.)
● 10:18–19
● 11:13
● 16:28
● 17:9
● 18:6–7
● 25:9–10
● 26:20

Then ask: 'Why are there so many references to gossip and slander in just one book? What does this suggest?' (Solomon, a wise man, regarded gossip and slander as dangerous.)

Also refer to:

Leviticus 19:16 – command not to spread slander.

Exodus 23:1 – do not spread false reports.

1 Timothy 5:13 – idleness and gossip often go together.

Romans 1:29–32 – gossip is listed along with other sins which include murder and ruthlessness. This shows the seriousness and destructive power of gossip.

RESPONDING TO GOSSIP (15 mins)

It's not enough just to tell people not to gossip. They need practice and strategies to know how to respond appropriately when someone is gossiping to them. Assign people to same-sex small groups of twos or threes and hand each group a photocopy of the sheet below and a pen. Tell them they have to think of an appropriate response to the gossipy situations on the sheet. The blank speech bubble is for them to write down a sentence or two in response. At the bottom of the sheet are a few ideas and strategies which they might like to employ. Encourage the groups to talk through ideas for appropriate responses. Tell them the aim is to avoid gossip without unnecessarily upsetting the gossiper or appearing like a goody-goody!

Allow the groups up to seven minutes to complete the sheet and then ask for feedback. Identify good responses and creative strategies, as well as talking through what the groups think would work best. Also spend some quality time talking about their responses to the questions at the bottom of the sheet.

You will need to spend some time preparing for their responses to questions 2 and 3. Some of your group may currently be struggling with this situation. Quite possibly they are the victims of gossip from others within the youth group! Lead this section sensitively and suggest that at some time we have all been guilty of spreading gossip as well as being on the receiving end.

It may be appropriate to spend a few moments of quiet together as a group, asking God's forgiveness for having gossiped about others. As well as confessing to God, encourage the group to find time at the end of the meeting to go over and quietly say 'sorry' and ask forgiveness of other group members, if God has shown them.

It may be helpful to read out the parable of the unforgiving debtor (Matthew 18:21–35) to highlight the point that God has forgiven us so much, therefore we must forgive others who have wronged us. Make the point that our forgiveness is conditional upon us forgiving others (Matthew 6:14–15).

Think of a positive response to the gossips, then write it down in the speech bubble. Try to identify words and phrases which will stop the person gossiping, without you offending them or seeming 'holier than thou'. Listed at the bottom are a few general strategies in responding to gossip which might give you an idea which you can phrase as a suitable response.

Have you heard about who Sanjay got off with last week?

You must have heard about whether Thomas is going to be expelled — he's your cousin. So what's going to happen to him? Are his mum and dad going to appeal against the decision?

...then Jenny told me that she didn't really like Danny, because he's got weedy legs, but she goes round his house so she can see his older brother Jeff. She reckons he's gorgeous and that he's got a tattoo of a mermaid on his bum...

Alice told you about her mum and dad splitting up. I know she did, 'cos she told me she did. But I bet you don't know why. Well, my sister told me she saw Alice's mum coming out of the Queen's Head last night with Mr Robson, the deputy head. Old Robbo is always eyeing up the girls in his tutor group, according to Sandy and Melissa. Do you reckon it's true about him and Alice's mum then?

ANTI-GOSSIP STRATEGIES AND IDEAS...

Change the subject – start talking about something positive and non-gossipy.

Confront – politely but firmly ask the person not to say any more on the subject

Disinterest – express your lack of interest in the subject, but try to be polite.

Shutdown – quickly end the conversation and/or leave (easiest down the phone).

Resolution – explain that you are trying hard not to be a gossip. Ask the person to help you by not tempting you to gossip.

Protect – if the gossip centres around a person (it usually does), defend their reputation and their right not to have people gossip behind their back.

1) How can you keep friends if you don't join in their gossip?

2) How should you respond when you are the victim of other people's gossip?

3) How should you respond when you have been gossiping about another person?

EXAM PRESSURE

MEETING AIM: To enable your group to recognise where exam pressure comes from – and how to deal with it.

WHAT A GAS! (10 mins)

You need two volunteers and a can of fizzy drink per round. Alternatively, use sparkling mineral water so the end results are less sticky!

Give them a word and ask them to respond with the first word that comes into their heads without hesitating or repeating your word. Throw in words like exams, maths and school to get them thinking. If they hesitate or repeat your word, they shake their can hard for five seconds. Three faults and their opponent gets to open the can at them! N.B. Take great care with this stunt, ensure that eyes and mouth are closed and that the stream of drink is not aimed at the area of the eyes. Also, this is not a good idea if the floor is carpeted!

KNOTTED UP (10 mins)

Get your group into threes. Hand out thin wire coat hangers and get your group to make a wire sculpture, depicting how they feel about exams and revision. Allow five minutes for sculpting and then display each creation, asking the group to explain the symbolism.

Make the point that not all pressure is bad. 'Fizz' is put into drinks under pressure and the can keeps the pressure on. If it didn't, the drink would go flat. Likewise, coat hangers are built to withstand stress. A degree of pressure can improve our performance – there's nothing like a deadline to get you working. Problems come when the pressure gets too much – the drink explodes, the coat hanger gets out of shape, and we feel we can't cope.

EXAM FEELINGS (5–10 mins)

If you have a group who like to draw you could do this section as well as or instead of 'Knotted Up'. Hand out photocopies of the sheet opposite along with felt-tipped pens, and ask everyone to do a drawing depicting the way they feel about exams. Allow up to four minutes for drawing and expression, then pin them on the wall/notice board and ask individuals to talk about what they have drawn and why. You could then use these sheets to get the adults in your church praying for the young people who face exams. Ask permission of the 'artists' first, then write down the names of any young person who is taking an exam in the coming months and then hand out the drawings to different members of your congregation. Ask them to put the drawing on their fridge, by their mirror or somewhere else in their house where it will be noticed and prompt prayer for those names listed.

BETTER THAN, WORSE THAN (10 mins)

Get your group – on paper – to complete this sentence in three different ways: Doing exams is better than _____ but worse than _____. For example: 'Doing exams is better than going to the dentist but worse than going to McDonald's.'

Get them to read out their answers. From that you can gauge how they feel about exams. Bear in mind the peer pressure that will be in operation! No one wants to be labelled a 'swot', and it's generally accepted that 'exams are awful' when in fact some might enjoy the challenge. Highlight that everyone is different and will feel differently about them, and that's OK.

USE YER BRAIN (10 mins)

Read: Luke 2:41–52. Jesus is enjoying using his brain, talking with older, wiser people and asking them questions. He is ready and keen to learn.

In verse 52 the NIV says: 'Jesus grew in wisdom and stature, in favour with God and in favour with men [people].' Jesus was not just clever – we are told that he grew in four areas:

● In wisdom – intellectually;
● In stature – physically;
● In favour with God – spiritually;
● In favour with people – socially.

To be balanced, we need to grow in those four areas. It's not enough to be an intellectual genius if you're unfit and unhealthy and can't relate to people. It's not enough to have a body like Hunter or Lightning if you aren't developing your relationship with God. We need to be balanced people.

Get a four-legged chair or stool with one leg that comes off. Illustrate how unbalanced their lives become when one or more areas are neglected.

Say: 'Academic work is important. You need to do your best and will probably need to spend more time when exams approach. But don't let it get out of proportion to the other three.'

PRESSURE POINTS (10–15 mins)

Brainstorm why they feel under pressure over exams. Their answers will probably fall into the following categories below. Try to give them tools to help them cope with each type of pressure. If your budget allows, give them something to remind them of the antidote to the pressure.

● **Revision**
Will they be able to understand, remember and apply everything they have covered?

Antidote: good study skills or 'eating elephants' ('How do you eat an elephant? One bite at a time').

Make a revision plan; break down the 'I've got to revise everything' feeling into manageable, achievable tasks; ask for help when they need it; take breaks during revision and relax; do sample questions. Buy some school and study books.

Give them a pen, eraser or something they can use in their revision.

● **Parents' and carers' expectations**
This will vary, but sometimes Christian families put massive pressure on to achieve.

Antidote: get them to talk regularly to parents (carers) about how they feel about exams and how to help. Tell them to reassure their parents (carers) that they'll do their best. Consult parents (carers) on revision times.

Give them a card for them to write to their parents (carers), updating them on how it's going.

● **Being awarded a grade which defines you for the rest of your life!**
Our worth doesn't depend on what qualifications we have, but it often feels like it does in August when results are published. They may feel that's the only chance, and if they blow it they'll have ruined their whole lives.

Antidote: finding a sense of worth, value and purpose in God and realising how much he loves them. Even people at genius level need to have their sense of value rooted in God.

Two things need to be kept in balance. God created us all unique and wants us to fulfil our potential. But he doesn't stop loving us and is still able to use us even when we don't get 'good' results.

Give them a card with Psalm 23 on it. Get them to put it where they can read it every day.

● **Friends!**
It's easy to compare ourselves to our friends with regard to revision times, grades, etc. Friends sometimes panic and pressurise each other, when they should support each other.

Antidote: realising they are individuals. They will each have their own pace of work (number of hours of revision is not the same as amount learned). Tell them to look out for each other. Plan time off together to let their hair down and relax.

Give them a bunch of grapes to remind them they need to stick together as a group!

EXTRA CARE

Here are some more ideas to encourage and support the young people in your group:
● Ring them before the exams they are particularly dreading;
● Invite them round to your house for a coffee and short revision break;
● Pray for them all each day, or each week;
● Be available when they feel they can't cope;
● Organise a party when the exams are over.

DEMON DRINK?

MEETING AIM: This meeting is primarily intended for those trying, or getting into pubs ie age 15+. It aims to teach what the Bible says about alcohol and about peer pressure to drink. Don't let them glaze over because they think you're into 'Preaching No!' mode.

'THE WHOLE TRUTH' (20+ mins)

When it comes to drink, advertisers only paint one picture; young, trendy and sexy. So get a video camera, then write, direct and film your own short, truthful advert about the other side of drinking. Pavement pizzas, pretend punch-ups, staggering penniless drunks, hangovers etc. should figure highly. If that sounds macho, try giggly tipsy girlies getting off with dodgy guys. But tell them to keep it Certificate 12 please! Alternatively, this could be used as a follow-up exercise which takes up the whole of next week's meeting.

NAME THAT DRINKER (10–15 mins)

Hand out pens and photocopies of the sheet opposite. Get the young people to work through the list in pairs, then get feedback on what they wrote.

Then ask them to list, in order of importance, the reasons why they think these particular brands sell well among young people.
● Advertising makes it look well trendy
● The bottle looks and feels cool
● The alcoholic strength (alcohol by volume) impresses
● It tastes better than any other
● Your mates drink it
● It's associated with hard-core drinkers and partyers
● Drunkenness guaranteed!

LIQUOR LANGUAGE (10 mins)

Church can sometimes be accused of being a culture with its own language that excludes outsiders. The drinking culture also has its 'in' phrases. All of these have a meaning. First, see if they know what they are, then come up with your own more amusing versions – eg:
● Whisky Chaser (Your dad running to get to the off-licence at 9.59 on a Saturday night!)
● Half-cut (Your brother's sad 'stepped' hairstyle)
● On the Wagon
● Down the Hatch
● Hair of the Dog
● Tanked Up
● Amber Nectar
● What's your poison?
● Happy Hour
● Out of his face

WHAT IF? (10 mins)

Ask the young people to break into small groups to discuss and report back on the issues raised below. Say: 'You will now have an impression of how alcohol is integrated into most teenage lifestyles. Even Christians think nothing of 'doing' God on Sundays, but 'doing' lager on Fridays and Saturdays. People want to enjoy life, but should we do without alcohol?

'Earlier this century Prohibition was in force in America. This was the age of Moonshine, speak-easies and Al Capone. No alcohol could be publicly bought or sold. Today the same law applies in Islamic states.

'Many MPs believe that the law should be tightened to cut down on under-age drinking and other alcohol-related problems. Where should they start? How about jail sentences for those who persistently attempt the current under-18s sport of "Will I be served in the off-licence?" Or what about compulsory breathalysers at school registration?'

OK, so if that's ridiculous, what about:
● A ban on under-age drinking on the streets, or alcohol-free zones?
● Banning alcoholic lemonade and other similar new drinks, which many claim are aimed at young people?
● Three out of the big four UK soaps are centred on a pub. Should that change?

BIBLE IMBIBING (5 mins)

Say that some people are surprised that the Bible sometimes extols the virtues of wine.

A tithe of the abundance of the vineyards which God promised to bless was required as a Drink Offering to bring before God in the Old Testament. If God judged the land, the wine would dry up. If he didn't it would flow! (Deuteronomy 7:13, etc).

Paul encouraged Timothy to drink – a bit (1 Timothy 5:23) and it seems Paul could take it or leave it so long as his brothers weren't offended (Romans 14:21).

As for Jesus, he used wine in his stories. He obviously knows his stuff, by telling how old and new wines behave in the "new wineskins" passages. However, he talked about a culture of eating and drinking in Matthew 24:38 and Luke 17:28 that dulled people to impending judgement. He did not directly condemn drink though. In fact by saying "I am the Vine" in John 15, he was in danger of being misunderstood. Imagine if he had said: "I am the pub, you are the punters." I can just hear the hackles rising!

Although there is a lot we don't know about heaven, Jesus did say that we'll be sharing wine with him on that day. Also, we can't forget Jesus' first miracle. At a wedding reception in Cana Jesus turned a large quantity of water into wine. Also, from Matthew 11:19, we can see that he was accused of being a drunkard – though this was a lie.

Like many of God's best blessings, it is the abuse of it which does damage. In the case of alcohol, its failure is where right judgement and self-control go out the window. Boozing banishes brains!

DRUNK AND DISORDERLY (10 mins)

Get different members of the group to find and read out these Scripture passages which highlight the danger of alcohol.
● Genesis 9:21 – Noah
● Genesis 19:32–33 – Lot
● 1 Samuel 1:14 – Samuel.
● Esther 1:7–12; 7:2 – King Xerxes
● Matthew 14:6 – King Herod
● Proverbs 20:1; 23:30–32; 31:4 – Odes to unknown Revellers
● Isaiah 5:11, 22; 22:13, 28:1 28:7 56:12 – More odes to unknown revellers

Say: 'In all of these if God's people had said "whoa!" to their drinking, then God may not have delivered his "Woe" to their future!'

SUMMARY (3 mins)

It has to be said, and maybe your group will be forcefully telling you this, that drinking is often very enjoyable. It does not always turn you into a delinquent, and some of the best opportunities to talk about 'life, the universe and everything!' happen over a drink. But if it becomes a fulfilment in itself then Christians have sold themselves short.

Summarise by saying that God's people 'march to a different beat', and while Psalm 4:7 and Ephesians 5:18 both acknowledge the 'feel good' factor that comes with alcohol, they encourage us to press on into God for the blessings that truly matter. You'll also have more in your pocket and less in your waistline afterwards!

Don't condemn drinkers, but do leave them with a godly attitude to their little tipple, while reinforcing the law!

NAME THAT DRINKER...

As a broad generalisation, who drinks what?

1. Vodka . . . .

2. Champagne . . . .

3. Alone at home with a bottle of gin . . . .

4. Special Brew . . . .

5. Homebrew . . . .

6. Alcoholic Blackcurrant . . . .

7. Vintage wines from particular vineyards . . . .

8. The cheapest own-brand lager . . . .

9. Scotch Whisky . . . .

10. 2-litre bottles of strong cider . . . .

11. Rum & fruit flavours in trendy 200ml bottles . . . .

12. Beaujolais Nouveau . . . .

13. Sherry from cut-glass decanters . . . .

14. Thick syrupy liqueur . . . .

15. Guinness . . . .

Agree on those alcoholic drinks that teenagers drink and write down the top five most popular brand names.

1) . . . .

2) . . . .

3) . . . .

4) . . . .

5) . . . .

CONSEQUENCES

MEETING AIM: To illustrate the truth of Galatians 6:7, that 'A man reaps what he sows'; and to make the group think hard about what their own lives are likely to produce. It's designed for a group with some Christian commitment, but if the last section is adapted it could be used with not-yet-Christians.

PREPARATION

Before the meeting, buy a girls' magazine which includes a simple 'photostory'. Cut out the frames and rearrange them, stuck down with blu-tak on a large sheet in a random order. If you have a large group, prepare two or three rearranged photostories.

AND SO (15 mins)

Arrange the group in a circle, and say you are going to begin telling them a story. But you won't complete it. Instead, at some point you will say 'And so…' and the next person in the circle must take it up from there. He or she must contribute at least three sentences, and then at any time can suddenly say 'And so…', passing the story on to the next person. Aim to get all the way around the circle before the story ends. Then discuss:
● Who made the most unexpected twist in the story?
● Who added the cleverest touch – tying lots of previous details together?
● Did the story end as you would have expected it to?

Say: 'Stories depend on consequences. In life, we expect one thing to grow out of another – A and so B, and so C. It's the same in life; all events have causes and consequences.' Give the group your rearranged photostory, and see if they can put the frames in their proper order. (If you have two or more, turn it into a speed contest.) Then, when it's complete, analyse what they did. How did they know which frame came after which? By looking at causes and consequences.

ACORNS AND OAKS (10 mins)

But which causes lead to which consequences? Divide into smaller groups, and give each sub-group one of these case studies to look at. Ask them to report back:
● What were the most important causes of the disaster in this story?
● What were the contributing causes?
● Which human being was most to blame?
● What could have happened which would have prevented the disaster?

DISASTER 1: THE CHARGE OF THE LIGHT BRIGADE

It is 1854, and the British Army is fighting the Crimean War. The Heavy Brigade have just attacked a large force of Russian cavalry, and completely routed them.

Officers of the Light Brigade, led by Lord Lucan, are envious; they would have liked a share in the glory.

Lucan is an unpleasant, disdainful character, who is hardly speaking to his brother-in-law, Lord Cardigan, his fellow officer in the Light Brigade.

The Russians have retreated behind a solid line of cannon at the end of a valley. Other Russian guns, in the hills, are being pulled away to safety as the Russians retreat. Lord Raglan, the British commander, sends an order to Lord Lucan, asking him to advance on the enemy and prevent them taking away their guns. But the order is unclear, and Lucan queries it. The messenger points vaguely down the valley, and Lucan takes it to mean that he is to charge directly against the line of cannon. It sounds suicidal, but Lucan is too arrogant a man to argue.

He commands Cardigan to line up for the charge. Cardigan protests, but Lucan cuts him short and rides off. Cardigan is too proud to make an issue of it.

As the charge begins, the original messenger realises the Brigade is heading the wrong way, and tries to stop Cardigan. Russian shrapnel kills him before he can. The Brigade charges into the withering Russian fire, and 329 out of 600 are dead. Nothing has been gained.

DISASTER 2: THE CLERK WHO COST LLOYDS $32 MILLION

Marc Colombo, 28, was an exchange dealer at Lloyds Bank's smallest overseas branch – Lugano, in Switzerland. Every day he watched the world's currencies changing their value on the foreign exchange market, and eventually he decided he knew how to make some money out of it. So in September 1974 he tried making a deal. He could do this because the bank never checked on the dealings of foreign exchange clerks.

On the bank's behalf, he contracted to buy 34 million US dollars at a time when he thought the dollar's value would go down. But it went up instead, and he had lost $1 million of the bank's money. Since his salary was only $9,000, he couldn't pay it back; instead he continued trading. Within nine months he had set up transactions worth $4,580 million, but he still couldn't cover his losses. The bank manager, who had no idea what Colombo was doing, continued to sign pieces of paper for him, naïvely believing that everything was in order.

Eventually, by complete chance (a casual remark from a senior French banker to a Lloyds boss in London) the operation was discovered and Colombo was arrested. The bank found, to its horror, that Colombo had committed them to risking a sum greater than the combined capital and reserves of all three banks in Switzerland. It took three weeks to sort out the damage, and still, after that, $32 million was lost.

What had gone wrong? He said, 'There was the pride of the foreign exchange dealer who will not admit failure… I was a prisoner of events.' The judge accepted that he had not been trying to make money for himself. He was fined $300 and given an 18-month suspended sentence.

(If you prefer, you could find up-to-date 'disaster' stories in the news, and substitute them.)

DAVID'S DISASTER (15 mins)

Compare results. Point out that although chance occurrences can affect the result (eg the messenger killed by shrapnel, or the fluctuations in the money market), human decisions have a lot to do with the consequences we suffer. We sow… then we reap. Read Galatians 6:7–10 (and if you can, have it written out on a flipchart or OHP acetate, so that it's permanently in view). The Bible illustrates this hundreds of times – one story is in 2 Samuel 11:1–27. Read the story aloud (they won't be bored with this one!), then hand out pens, copies of the sheet opposite and divide into groups. Allow ten minutes for them to complete the questions then get feedback.

THIS IS YOUR FUTURE? (15 mins)

Go back to Galatians 6:7–9 and remind the group of what it says, pointing out that one chapter earlier, Paul described what it meant to 'sow to please our sinful nature' and to 'sow to please the Spirit'. Read Galatians 5:19–23, then give everyone a piece of paper with the following headings:
BAD SEED
● Impure sexual behaviour or thoughts
● Worshipping something else more than God
● Hating, fighting or envying other people
● Losing control, being self-indulgent or getting drunk
GOOD SEED
● Love ● Joy ● Peace ● Patience ● Kindness
● Goodness ● Faithfulness ● Gentleness
● Self-control

Ask them to think over what they have done in the last seven days, and to put a tick next to any 'seed' that they have planted. When have they shown patience, or reliability, or God's love? When have they given in to envy, jealousy or self-indulgence? What will the fruit of their life be if they go on planting as they are at the moment?

Ask them also to work out:
● What subjects dominate your thoughts most of the time?
● What's the biggest ambition you have? What would please you more than anything else in the world?
● Who don't you get on with, and why?
● Where do you struggle most with self-discipline – chocolate? laziness? spending money? the opposite sex? Are you winning or losing?

Finally, ask them to think of one thing they would like to be said about them after they have died. (Example: Eric Delve once remarked: 'Whatever else my kids say about me, I hope they will say, "My Dad knew God."')

Depending on the closeness of your group, you may wish to ask them to share some of their thoughts and discoveries with one other person, and then pray together. Or you may wish them to pray over in silence, individually, what God is saying to them through the self-examination they have just done. Make sure you end on a note of triumph – not guilty introspection! – making the point that God's Spirit lives in us to help us yield a triumphant harvest of righteousness. Our potential is infinite!

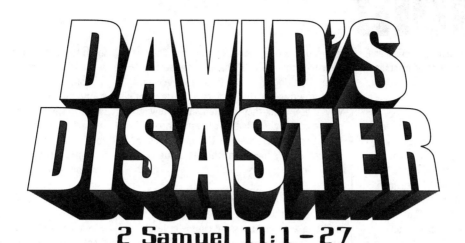

DAVID'S DISASTER

2 Samuel 11:1 - 27

1. Verse 1 gives you a hint about why David was vulnerable to temptation. Can you see what it is?

....

....

2. David wasn't just wicked himself – he implicated other people in doing evil. Who?

....

....

3. Which of these principles are true, according to this story?
- If you commit just one sin, you'll get away with it.
- One evil deed leads inevitably on to another.
- It can be difficult to disentangle yourself from evil once you have become involved.
- It's all right to sleep with women if their husbands die shortly afterwards.

4. Doing evil always exacts a heavy cost. What price did David have to pay in military terms?

....

....

5. Later, David did what was right (12:13–14). But even after we repent, the consequences of evil may continue. What were they (12:15–18)?

....

....

6. And there was more to come. Skim through the story in chapter 13. Does this have any connection with David's sin in chapter 11? And does anybody remember what the ultimate consequences were for Absalom (in chapter 18:33)?

....

....

SEXISM

MEETING AIM: To explore the subject of sexism and give young people a greater understanding of the issues involved.

INTRODUCTION

This is a big subject, and it's one where feelings usually run high! Different churches have different practices. For example, in some places women aren't allowed to preach. You need to be able to explain things that might appear to the young people to be sexist. Why does your church do it that way? This session is not meant to be divisive. Your instinct might be to leave this topic alone, but if your church do prescribe roles, your young people need to understand the reasons why.

SECOND-CLASS CITIZENS (2 mins)

As the young people arrive, treat the boys differently from the girls. Laugh, joke and share your polos with the boys, and tell the girls to sit quietly (or vice versa!).

WILLY PREACHIT (10 mins)

Get some of your group to perform the sketch opposite as a way of introducing the theme of sexism.

Get your group's immediate reactions to the sketch.

Say: 'We're looking at the topic of sexism today – what it is, and what it isn't. That was why we ignored some of you as you arrived – to give you an understanding of how it feels to be treated as second class. The sketch was an extreme example of men and women being given different roles at a church event. We'll be looking at why that happens and whether it's right or wrong.'

WHO DOES WHAT? (15 mins)

Make photocopies of the worksheet opposite. Hand them out with pens to your group. Allow five minutes for them to complete the blanks. Be sensitive to those from one-parent families, and make the point that single parents don't have any choice about what they contribute to keeping the household going.

Discuss the results. Are there different roles in your family? Does it matter? Do boys and girls get treated differently? Is that fair? Why are there differences at church? What would happen if roles were swapped over? Is any of this sexist? What about language used at church (refer back to sketch)?

Does the use of the word 'men' or 'mankind' still refer to men and women (ask the girls which toilets they use – chances are they don't go in the ones marked 'men'!)? Be prepared to answer the question, 'Why is church like this?'!

Make the point that these sheets are getting you to look at your experiences. The roles we grow up with shape our expectations. That doesn't mean these are necessarily right or wrong, or that they have to stay that way. If you think that 'women should always do the cooking', is that just because no one else in your house does it? However roles are shared out, it's important that we value each other's contribution.

GENDER GUIDE (15–20 mins)

Covering all the biblical material on gender would take an eight-session course at least! This study gives a foundation from which to look at the more 'difficult' passages.

Ask them to retell the story of the creation of men and women, and the fall (when they disobeyed God and ate the fruit). Why was Eve made? Where was Adam when Eve ate the fruit? What happened as a result of the fall? Read Genesis 2:4–9 15–25, and Genesis 3. Then make the following points:

1) After creating each thing, God saw that it was good (chapter 1). In Genesis 2:18, for the first time something is not good – the fact that man was alone. God makes a helper. The word means someone to complement him. Imagine trying to use a two-handled saw to cut a huge tree trunk. It would be impossible to do it on your own. You need a 'helper', someone who can work with you, playing their part, to get the job done.

2) Adam was with Eve when she ate the fruit, so he was just as responsible. It wasn't only her fault! Both man and woman disobeyed God.

3) The relationship before the fall is one of equality. Adam calls Eve 'bone of my bone, flesh of my flesh' – in other words, 'You're just like me!' God gave to both men and women the task of looking after the earth and having babies (Genesis 1:27–28). After the fall, God describes the kind of relationships they'll now have. Genesis 3:16 says, 'Your desire will be for your husband and he will rule over you.' That's where competition and being bossy comes in. It wasn't part of God's original plan.

Jesus was born in a time when women were not well treated. They weren't taught, and were considered to be the possessions of their fathers or husbands. Jewish men were forbidden to talk to women in public. Pharisees would pray, 'Thank you, God, that I am not a woman or a Gentile.' Look up these passages to see how Jesus treated women:
● Mary and Martha (Luke 10:38–42; gave Mary a chance to learn).
● Woman at the well (John 4:4–26; taught a Samaritan woman).
● Women followers (Luke 8:1–3; allowed them to support him).
● Martha's confession (John 11:27; parallels that of Peter in Luke 9:20).
● Anointed by the prostitute (Luke 7:36–40; much to the horror of his host).
● Mary at the tomb (Matthew 28:1–10; culture didn't allow women to be witnesses in court, yet Jesus allowed them to be the first to see him alive).

WHAT IS SEXISM? (10–15 mins)

Ask your group to come up with a definition of sexism. A good one is: 'Attitudes or actions that discriminate against women or men on grounds of gender'.

Have any of them suffered from sexist attitudes or actions? How did they feel at the start of the session when you were discriminating against them according to gender? Both men and women can be victims of sexism. Attitudes can be as painful to experience as actions.

Make the point that different treatment of the sexes isn't necessarily sexist. Sexism is unfair treatment. For example, girls may feel or be less safe out at night, so they need lifts home.

Boys or girls may never have had the opportunity to do an activity because traditionally it has 'belonged' to the other sex. They may need extra encouragement to have a go.

One gender may particularly enjoy a sport that doesn't appeal to the other. That doesn't mean sport shouldn't be played, or that everything has to appeal to everyone.

This might be the place to discuss why your church does things in a certain way, but make sure you have a sound biblical argument, and you're not simply attempting to justify sexism!

WHAT ABOUT ME? (5 mins)

None of us likes to think we're prejudiced, until we discover that we are! Take some time to reflect as individuals and as a group about whether you are sexist.

Ask them what they think about the youth group. Are any of your activities or ways of relating sexist? Listen to what they have to say.

Get them to examine themselves. Are they sometimes 'conveniently' sexist, for example not offering to help with the washing up because the girls always do it. What do they need to put right?

Conclude with prayer, asking God to forgive us and help us to change our attitudes and actions so that we value one another.

CHARACTERS: Willy Preachit, Arthur Chorus and two anonymous women.

Willy and Arthur are dressed in (old) suits and are thanking everyone at the end of a church Bible week.

WILLY: Shall we pray? Father God, Magnificent Warrior and Mighty King, we praise you for our church Bible week because you have richly blessed these brothers with your presence. Thank you for these anointed men of God who have ministered to us this week. Send us out, we pray, as soldiers of your Kingdom to fight the good fight and lead all men everywhere to know you. Amen.

ARTHUR: Thank you for attending this week of ministry. We trust you have been richly blessed. We want to take this opportunity to say a few thank-you's. First, to a man who's led many men to the Lord — Dr Willy Savem. A real man of God — thank you brother for your ministry of the word.

WILLY: We'd also like to thank the Happy Clappy Drama group and the Moony Swoony Dance Ensemble for their Christian Morris Dancing — all great guys with great gifts.

ARTHUR: A big thank-you to our wonderful male voice choir, The Everso Shiny Brighty Lighty Singing Group. And especially to our dear old soloist who's been a real inspiration to us over the years — Mr George Heavily Shaved.

WILLY: Thank you to Mr Bernard Goatee for lending us the hall, and to the wonderful team of technicians and lighting crew led by Mr Sly Manoeuvres.

ARTHUR: And to you, of course, Mr Willy Preachit, for your masterful chairmanship.

WILLY: And to you, Arthur, for your great worship leading qualities. Gentlemen, Mr Arthur Chorus.

ARTHUR: *(slight pause)* Oh…and we mustn't forget to thank the wives who've released these men into their ministries, and to our dear sisters who've worked so hard behind the scenes. Because as we all know — behind every great man is a great woman.

WILLY: And so we shall end our time together by singing that old hymn — a real challenge to us men of God — 'He who would valiant be, 'gainst all disaster, let him with constancy follow the master'.

Arthur and Willy assume worship positions with closed eyes and freeze. 'Sisters are doing it for themselves' by Eurythmics begins, loud. Two girls enter, sweeping floor in time to music. They cut the boys' trouser legs, rip off their ties, plaster them in shaving foam and generally humiliate them. They leave and the music fades. Men open eyes and look bemused.

WILLY: What do you make of that, then?

ARTHUR: Must be the time of the month!

A. Who does what in your home?

	Always Men	Mostly Men	About Equal	Mostly Women	Always Women
1) washing clothes	☐	☐	☐	☐	☐
2) gardening	☐	☐	☐	☐	☐
3) cooking barbecues	☐	☐	☐	☐	☐
4) organising holidays	☐	☐	☐	☐	☐
5) cooking meals	☐	☐	☐	☐	☐
6) walking the dog	☐	☐	☐	☐	☐
7) car maintenance	☐	☐	☐	☐	☐
8) washing up	☐	☐	☐	☐	☐
9) shopping for food	☐	☐	☐	☐	☐
10) DIY — fixing things in house	☐	☐	☐	☐	☐
11) paying the bills/finances	☐	☐	☐	☐	☐
12) redecorating	☐	☐	☐	☐	☐
13) cleaning the car	☐	☐	☐	☐	☐
14) ironing	☐	☐	☐	☐	☐
15) putting out rubbish	☐	☐	☐	☐	☐

B. Who does what in your church?

	Always Men	Mostly Men	About Equal	Mostly Women	Always Women
1) leading worship	☐	☐	☐	☐	☐
2) teaching Sunday school	☐	☐	☐	☐	☐
3) putting out chairs	☐	☐	☐	☐	☐
4) making decisions	☐	☐	☐	☐	☐
5) preaching sermons	☐	☐	☐	☐	☐
6) leading the prayers	☐	☐	☐	☐	☐
7) welcoming people	☐	☐	☐	☐	☐
8) organising creche	☐	☐	☐	☐	☐
9) serving coffee after church	☐	☐	☐	☐	☐
10) visiting people during the week	☐	☐	☐	☐	☐
11) cleaning the church	☐	☐	☐	☐	☐
12) leading the service	☐	☐	☐	☐	☐
13) running parent and toddler group	☐	☐	☐	☐	☐
14) running the youth group	☐	☐	☐	☐	☐
15) doing the flowers	☐	☐	☐	☐	☐

ABSOLUTES

MEETING AIM: To help young people see that they are living in a culture where absolute values are anathema, and relativism rules; that nonetheless absolutes are vital, and that God has given us some non-negotiable principles which we water down at our peril. Despite this description, it isn't intended to be an academic, philosophical session, but one that enables young people to reflect practically on the decisions they make and the reasons for their choices.

WHATEVER TURNS YOU ON (10 mins)

Select three group members and get them to play an exhibition game of Monopoly (or Scrabble or anything else suitable) in front of the others.

Tell them that there's just one different rule: whenever someone throws a four, that player is allowed to do whatever he wants (eg move the other players' pieces, award himself triple points for the round, start playing Snakes and Ladders instead – but don't give them too many ideas; let them dream them up for themselves).

The result will be chaos, resentment and probably a quick end to the game, as somebody realises that on throwing a four he can simply declare the game over and award himself the victory!

(If you have a large group, and a board game isn't visual enough, you could play a team game of any kind your group like, suspending the rules for 30 seconds every time a hooter is suddenly blown. Once again, this should produce chaos, uncertainty and arguments!)

Say: 'To make a game happen, we need rules which don't alter. Progress is impossible if suddenly the basic rules are likely to change. It's the same in society – we need fixed laws to ensure our freedom. Would you feel more or less happy to walk outside at night if your next-door neighbour could blast you with a shotgun, because laws against murder had just changed? And it's the same in our personal lives. We need fixed values, called "absolutes", to determine our conduct by.'

WHERE TO NEXT? (5 mins)

Produce an electric jigsaw and a piece of scrap chipboard. For safety's sake, bring some goggles too, and supervise this activity closely! Ask a couple of people to cut a perfect circle in the wood. Unless they're very skilful (choose people who aren't!), they'll find it impossible. Then fix the metal guide to the saw, and show how it's easy to cut a circle when there's a fixed guide, firmly moored to one point from which it doesn't move. It's hard to know which way the saw should go without a fixed reference point; it's hard to know which way our lives should go without

absolutes.

(No good at carpentry? Find a tradesman or DIY-er in the church to do this bit for you!)

GOD'S FIXED POINTS (10 mins)

Now do a bit of Bible study to discover what some of God's absolutes are. Explain that some commands in the Bible apply to just one stage of history, and others are absolutes for all time. Ask them to sort out which are which in this list:

Exodus 21:28
Deuteronomy 23:24
Deuteronomy 5:17
Exodus 20:14
Deuteronomy 14:19
Exodus 20:15
Deuteronomy 22:11

Then ask: 'Why do we regard some as unchanging, and others as temporary?'

It's because some are vital principles that apply in every culture at every time, and God keeps on reminding us of them right the way through Scripture – while others are dropped or changed (Matthew 5:33–34, 38–39). Absolutes like truth, love, purity and selflessness are basic because they reflect the character of God himself. We're made to be this way.

SHIFTING THE GOALPOSTS (10 mins)

Brainstorm together a list of the most important absolutes God has given us. Write up suggestions on an OHP or whiteboard and vote on the top ten. Then divide into smaller groups. Give each group two or three absolutes to think about, and ask them to suggest messages within our culture – song lyrics, films, soap plots, etc – which demonstrate how differently today's society thinks about these principles. Ask them to think about the behaviour of non-Christian friends at school or college. How would these friends rewrite God's principles?

Point out that we live in a culture where people think of absolutes as harsh, inhuman and intolerant. But as we saw at the start, where there are no rules there is chaos. There wouldn't be so many miserably broken families if we took God's sexual and marital absolutes seriously. Things in the shops wouldn't cost so much if people valued honesty more highly.

IT ALL DEPENDS (15 mins)

That doesn't mean it's always easy to make moral decisions. Situations can be complicated, mainly through human sin. But there's usually an absolute principle, in any situation, to guide our thinking.

Hand out pens and copies of the sheet opposite, one between two or three. Each

small group must decide what absolutes might apply in these tricky situations. (It's probable that the group won't be completely agreed about what should happen in these cases! But they should be able to see the underlying, absolute principles on which a decision must be based. It isn't just a case of 'doing what you feel like'; there are guidelines.)

Allow them 10 minutes then get them to feed back and discuss.

THIS MEANS YOU (10 mins)

It's important for us not just to agree mentally, but to discipline ourselves to live by God's absolutes too. Sometimes it can be hard. What advice would the group give to Christians with the following problems?

● 'I must be the only virgin left in my year. It's so tough when everybody pities you and accuses you of being frigid or homosexual or something. And all the sexual stuff in films and on TV and in adverts makes it worse. Is it worth the struggle?'

● 'I know marijuana's an illegal drug. But surely we know now it's less dangerous than alcohol. It's sheer hypocrisy that makes people ban it when you can get smashed out of your brains on booze. And it's brilliantly relaxing. I've got to pass those exams.'

● 'Anybody who says you have to love your parents just hasn't met my dad.'

How do we gain the strength to live by God's absolutes? Divide the group into threes, and give each small group one of these passages:

Romans 6:11–14;
Philippians 1:27–30;
Colossians 3:15–17.

Ask them to read the passage and then, within two minutes, come up with at least one practical survival suggestion from their passage. (There are loads! You may wish to bring out some of those they don't spot.)

Pool your ideas, and close in prayer, thanking God for his unchanging, reliable character, and asking him for strength to live consistently and powerfully in the way he has planned.

IT ALL DEPENDS...

Read out the situations and talk about what the main character should do. It may be that you won't be able to agree completely about what should happen, but try to identify the underlying, absolute principles on which a decision must be based. It isn't just a case of 'doing what you feel like'; there are guidelines. You have three minutes per dilemma...

A girl has become unexpectedly pregnant after a drunken fling at a party. She knows that her boyfriend will desert her if he knows. So she manages to seduce him and persuade him that the baby is his. Then he finds out about the party.

A junior manager in a retail firm finds out that senior employees are taking money out of the company, and hiding their dishonesty by overcharging customers. He is invited to join the scheme, and warned that he will be dismissed if he blows the whistle – '...and we'll see that you never work again in this industry.' He has a wife and three small children.

A doctor has a patient with a terminal complaint. The patient's wife has begged the doctor not to tell him that he is going to die, since it would plunge him into a deep depression and hasten the end. The patient comes to see the doctor and demands to know the truth.

ANIMAL RIGHTS

MEETING AIM: To introduce your group to the issues at stake in debates about animal rights, cruelty to animals, and human domination of creation. This outline works best with a group who are reasonably thoughtful and convinced of the authority of Scripture (although it can be adapted for other uses). It gives no easy answers about vegetarianism, animal experiments, battery farming, etc., but simply tries to point out the base beliefs on which Christians can start to work out their personal position. It should help Christians relate their faith to the arguments which rage in the average sixth form college common room.

CHECK IT OUT

To check out the territory before you start, there's a good (although inconclusive) chapter in *The Puzzle Of Ethics* by Vardy and Grosch (Fount). David Henshaw's *Animal Warfare: The Story Of The Animal Liberation Front* is worth reading. Andrew Linzey is the best Christian author on this subject (his writings are published by Grove and SPCK). Web sites include http://www.tiac.net/users/sbr/animals.html (animal health,well-being and rights); http://www.animal-law.org (Animal Rights Law Centre); http://labanimal.com/home.html (LabAnimal News, for scientists who use animals in experiments); http://www.hedweb.com/arfaq/arpage.htm (frequently asked questions on animal rights); and orbyss.com/animl1.htm (a link page for many animal rights groups). One brief Christian page is http://senet.com.au/hot/ww.htm#z.

GETTING STARTED

Photocopy and cut out the 'role cards' for The Cocktail Party. Photocopy the 'Human Rights' statement. Make a pack of cards for 'The Human Difference' containing six, each bearing these legends: 'Able to use tools'; 'Made to resemble God'; 'Namer and organiser of creation'; 'Breathing and living'; 'IQ of over 100'; 'Ruler of God's planet'; 'Able to write poetry'; 'Capable of personal relationships'; 'Formed out of the ground'; 'The final act of God's creation'.

THE COCKTAIL PARTY (15 mins)

Start by giving each group member one of the role cards from the photocopy sheet opposite. Tell them they're going to be this person for the next ten minutes. They've been invited to a cocktail party where they will mingle and chat with many other people – finding out their job, views on life, etc. They must try to speak to at least four other people in the time allotted.

Now hold the party! Call a halt before it

runs out of steam. Ask: did anyone:
a) get into a furious argument
b) have absolutely nothing in common
c) agree totally with someone else they talked to?

Get some reports. Ask the group: would these people have behaved like this in real life? Is this the sort of thing they would have said?

Conclude: the subject of animals is a complicated issue, and many people today have very strong feelings. It wasn't always like this. Have someone read out the opinion of Aristotle...

'Plants exist for the sake of animals, and brute beasts for the sake of man – domestic animals for his use and food, wild ones for food and other accessories of life, such as clothing and various tools'

...and the great philosopher Immanuel Kant:

'Animals are not self-conscious, and are there merely as a means to an end. That end is man.'

But today some feel so strongly about animal rights that they will poison human food and blow up cars, to protect them. On the other hand, some animals have been invented simply for our convenience (eg the mouse on which a giant ear has been cultivated; Dolly the cloned sheep; the 'superpig' which yields much more meat, but suffers arthritis, impotence and skull deformity).

In 1990 there were over three million animal experiments carried out in Britain, of which two million were performed without anaesthetic, 60,000 deliberately produced cancer, and less than half were for medical research reasons. What should Christians make of all that?

THE BIBLE ON BUDGIES (10 mins)

Divide into small groups. Read these verses: Luke 12:6; Genesis 1:28; Job 12:7–10; Proverbs 12:10; Deuteronomy 25:4. Now discuss what is wrong with these half-baked statements:
● 'According to Christianity, we can do anything we like to animals.'
● 'Animals aren't aware of God in any way.'
● 'Humans are just one more type of animal.'
● 'Animals are just accidental by-products in God's creation, so we can be as cruel as we like.'

Compare results. Say: 'The Bible doesn't say much about animals, but it reveals that they are a carefully planned and loved part of God's creation, and we have to be careful how we treat them. We have authority over them, and throughout the Bible that included using them for food and clothing. But we're responsible to God for our stewardship of his creation.'

YOU'RE IN CHARGE (15 mins)

But what does that mean we can and can't do? Christians disagree. Give each group a list of ten 'Human Rights' and ask them to decide which they agree with. Encourage them to refer to the Bible, wherever they can, in making their decisions. Allow plenty of time for this part as it can become quite heated!

Because I am a Christian, I have the right to...
● keep a pet;
● eat meat;
● experiment on rabbits, if humans will benefit in some way;
● experiment on rabbits, if it will make humans wealthier;
● wear furs;
● go foxhunting;
● kill spiders and wasps;
● run a safari park full of imprisoned animals;
● free battery hens and monkeys kept in cages;
● put down a mousetrap.

When you compare results, don't attempt to achieve total agreement on all those points, because you won't! Instead, look at how people approached the questions. What arguments were used? What principles were appealed to? Different Christians may arrive at different conclusions, but we should agree about the underlying principles.

Finally, ask: 'Do animals have any rights? What should they be?'

THE HUMAN DIFFERENCE (10 mins)

Say: 'The key to these issues is the difference between humans and animals.'

Read Genesis 1:26–30; 2:19–23. Let people think about it for a moment. Then give each group one card from the 'Human Difference' pack you've prepared (see above). Tell them to discuss together whether this is really one of the key things that makes humans different from animals. If so, they can keep it and take one more card from the pack. If not, they can discard it and take two more cards from the pack. They continue in turn, taking new cards and replacing those they don't want, until one group believes it has five 'correct' cards. If they're right, they've won. Give the winners a packet of jelly babies, and the losers Animal Bars.

PUTTING IT TOGETHER (5 mins)

Sum up all that has been learned about God's attitude to animals; the responsibility he expects from us; the position we occupy in his creation; the possibility of disagreement between Christians about the practical ways of working it out. Read Psalm 8 and let it sink in for a moment. Then pray together.

an animal liberation activist	a bee-keeper	someone who works in an abattoir	zoo-keeper
an enthusiastic vegetarian	a champion dog breeder	a bullfighter	a scientist who experiments on animals
a New Ager who believes all life is divine and must be respected	an Indian guru who believes all life is sacred and killing a fly is murder	a showjumper	an old woman who keeps lots of cats
a housewife who actively campaigns against the live export of animals for slaughter	a farmer who keenly supports foxhunting and other 'blood sports'	a manager of a burger bar	a butcher

I'LL BE THERE FOR YOU

MEETING AIM: Everyone needs friends around them to share the ups and downs of life, whether it's about falling in love, life at school or work or the trials and troubles of family life! But every now and then, someone may face a more serious crisis which threatens to overwhelm them.

How do you help a friend who feels suicidal, is struggling with depression, deep anxiety or an eating disorder? This sessions aims to encourage young people to take action when they see friends facing a crisis of this magnitude. So often the will to support them is already there; it's simply a matter of knowing how to go about helping.

Some thought will need to be given as to the suitability of this session for the age and background of your young people. The best results will come from adapting the material here to suit the young people you work with and leaving out anything that doesn't apply to your situation.

ER, EMERGENCY ROOM! (15 mins)

Set the scene by dividing into small groups of three or four and giving each group a scenario where one of their friends shares with them about a crisis they are going through. They have 10 minutes to work out how they would deal with the situation under four headings:

● How would you feel when you first heard about/discovered the crisis?
● What would you say to them to help them?
● What would you do to help them?
● Would you feel confident or inadequate about what you could do, and why?

1. You're sitting at home watching TV on your own when there's a knock at the door. As you open it, you see one of your friends standing there with tears streaming down their face. When you ask them what's wrong, they tell you that their parents have just announced that they're splitting up...

2. You've always wondered if one of your friends struggled with an eating disorder. One day you happen to go into the school toilets after lunch and walk straight into this friend stuffing laxative tablets down their throat. The room smells like someone's been sick too...

3. You're out for a walk with one of your friends when they confess to you that last week they thought about committing suicide because of the pressure they are under to do well at exams. They tell you that it all feels too much and, with their hassles at home as well, it doesn't seem worth going on.

4. After the death of one of their family, your friend has been feeling down for months. As you're sitting chatting during one lunchtime

break, they tell you that they've been to see the doctor for some anti-depressants, but nothing seems to help.

THIRD ROCK FROM THE SUN? (20+ mins)

Skilled counsellors able to deal with any situation without a hassle? Always having the right Bible verse to hand or knowing the right words to say at any moment? If this sounds like someone from another planet to your young people, this next section should reassure them you don't have to be perfect to help, but just what qualities are needed?

There are no absolute right and wrong answers to this challenge, but it does help young people think through what's important in helping out a friend in need. Put a large piece of paper up on the wall with the different qualities below written on it and ask the group to place them in order of how important they think they are when you're trying to help someone. Get them to report back to the others and discuss together why they chose that order.

● relationship with Jesus
● Bible knowledge
● humility
● knowledge of where to get help: advice lines, etc.
● no major problems yourself
● good at listening
● genuinely interested in helping
● been through the same experience
● ability to understand how others feel
● already good friends
● able to keep things confidential
● knowing when you're out of your depth

Finish this section by having an open time where young people can share their experiences either of struggling with some of these issues themselves (what helped? did you have friends who supported you?) or who have known someone who has faced them (what did you do to help? how did you feel?).

FRIENDS OR *FRASIER?* (15 mins)

Young people are not expected to be able to offer detailed advice and counselling to their friends. Instead they're there simply to show that person they are loved and cared for. If you want some light relief, try showing clips from the American sit-coms *Friends* and *Frasier* to illustrate the difference. (If either of these titles leaves you confused, ask one of your youth group!) 'Being there' and listening is often the most important role they can play. Take a look together at how Jesus spent time listening to and helping people in the example of Matthew 8:1–4 (where he healed the leper).

● What do you think were the implications of having leprosy in the way people treated you?
● What other issues provoke the same reaction in many people today? (AIDS, homosexuality, etc.)
● Why do you think Jesus touched the man?
● Who made the first approach: Jesus or the man with leprosy? Do you think this was important?

HOME IMPROVEMENT (5 mins)

It may be useful to give your young people some addresses and contacts they can follow up when they get home. They may want to get information in order to help themselves, or to help a friend.

One of the best ways to do this is to get some of your youth group to research both national and local groups themselves and report back.

In addition, photocopy the info sheet opposite and hand out for future reference.

Finish the session by reminding your young people that they are not expected to carry the burdens and hassles of all their friends. They should always be ready to support and encourage any of their friends facing a crisis, but they should also know when to involve someone with more experience and know-how. Ultimately our trust is in God to look after those in need. Try reading Psalm 42 before closing in prayer and asking together that God will give you all the courage and confidence to help those around you who are in the midst of a crisis.

USEFUL CONTACTS
(keep this in a safe place)
Please note: some but not all of these organisations are staffed by Christians.

ALCOHOL/DRUG-RELATED ISSUES
Hope UK, 25f Copperfield Street,
London SE1 0EN
Tel: 0171 928 0848

Alcohol Concern
305 Grays Inn Road, London WC1X 8QF
Tel: 0171 833 3471

ScoDA
1-4 Hatton Place, off Hatton Garden,
London EC1N 8ND
Tel: 0171 430 2341

TACADE
1 Hulme Place, The Crescent, Salford,
Lancashire M5 4QA
Tel: 0161 745 8925

Lifeline
101-103 Oldham Street, Manchester M4 1LW
Tel: 0161 839 2054

ABUSE-RELATED ISSUES
PCCA Christian Childcare
PO Box 133, Swanley, Kent BR8 7UQ
Tel: 01322 667207

National Society for the Prevention of
Cruelty to Children (NSPCC)
67 Saffron Hill, London EC1N 8RS
Tel: 0171 242 1626

BULLYING
Kidscape
152 Buckingham Palace Road,
London SW1W 9TR
Tel: 0171 730 3300

EATING DISORDERS
Eating Disorders Association
Sackville Place, 44-48 Magdalen Street,
Norwich NR3 1JE
Tel: 01603 621414

ADVICE & LEAFLETS ON LONELINESS, SUICIDE, BEREAVEMENT etc./24-HOUR HELPLINE
Crossline (Plymouth)
Methodist Central Hall, Eastlake Street,
Plymouth PL1 1BA
Tel: 01752 666777

NATIONAL REFERRALS TO LOCAL CHRISTIAN COUNSELLORS
CWR
Waverley Abbey House, Waverley Lane,
Farnham, Surrey GU9 8EP
Tel: 01252 783695

RUNAWAYS/HOUSING
Centrepoint
PO Box 405, London WC2H 8HD
Tel: 0171 379 3466

Young Men's Christian Association
640 Forest Road, London E17 3DZ
Tel: 0181 520 5599

Young Women's Christian Association
Clarenden House, 52 Cornmarket Street,
Oxford OX1 3EJ
Tel: 01865 726110

SEXUAL HEALTH
National AIDS helpline
PO Box 1577, London NW1 3DW
Tel: 0171 387 6900

TELEPHONE HELPLINES
Childline
Tel: 0800 1111
Samaritans
Tel: 0345 909090 (for local branches see entry
in your telephone directory)

SUPPORT FOR VICTIMS OF CRIME
Victim Support
Cranmer House, 39 Brixton Road, London SW9 6DZ
Tel: 0171 735 9166